MINIPEDIA
ON THE MOVE

D1516451

tangerine
Press

TANGERINE PRESS and associated designs are trademarks of Scholastic Inc.

Authors: Philip Wilkinson, Ian Graham, Howard Johnston, Ian Ward

A Marshall Edition
Produced by KINSEY & HARRISON for
Marshall Editions Ltd
Just House, 74 Shepherd's Bush Green, London W12 8QE, England
www.marshallpublishing.com

Copyright © 2002 Marshall Editions Developments, Ltd

Scholastic and Tangerine Press and associated logos are trademarks of
Scholastic Inc.

Published by Tangerine Press, an imprint of Scholastic Inc.;
555 Broadway, New York, NY 10012

10 9 8 7 6 5 4 3 2 1

ISBN 0-439-38192-4

Originated in the U.K. by Grasmere Digital Imaging
Printed and bound in Portugal by Printer Portuguesa

General Consultant: (and Wheels and Air)
Andrew Nahum, Senior Curator, Aeronautics and Road Transport, Science
Museum, London
Consultants: Tracks: Tim Bryan, Steam: Museum of the Great Western
Railway, Swindon; Water: Pieter van der Merwe, General Editor, National
Maritime Museum, Greenwich; Space: Douglas Millard, Associate Curator,
Space Technology, Science Museum, London
Indexer: Patricia Hymans

Designer: Edward Kinsey Editor: James Harrison

Marshall Editions
Design Managers: Ralph Pitchford, Caroline Sangster
Editorial Manager: Kate Phelps
Assistant Editor: Elise See Tai
Proofreader: Claire Sipi
Picture Researcher: Zilda Tandy
DTP Manager: Ali Marshall
Production: Anna Pauletti

Contents

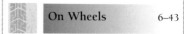

Introduction

Since the earliest times, people have traveled—to find food, to carry goods for trading, for sheer adventure, to find what is over the next hill or across the sea. To begin, they walked or rode animals, but they built the first boats in prehistoric times, and wheeled vehicles were first used 5,000 years ago.

For thousands of years these forms of transportation developed gradually. Boat-builders designed better sails and methods of steering their craft; different styles of cart and carriage were developed for land transport. These changes came slowly, but they had a huge effect. For example, better ships enabled people such as the Vikings to go on the first long-distance voyages of exploration, crossing the Atlantic in search of new places to settle. Again in the 15th and 16th centuries, European explorers used the latest ships to go huge distances, some even sailing right around the globe. But few people traveled that far. Most men and women did not go far beyond their immediate neighborhoods, and if they did travel long distances, the journey was likely to be slow, difficult, and dangerous.

Woodburner

Viking longship

Then, in the 19th century, a change took place which transformed transportation for good. Engineers in Europe developed the railroad, bringing fast, safe land transportation within the reach of many people for the first time.

Railroads also allowed goods to be transported faster and more efficiently than ever before, helping industry and making people less reliant on food and other items produced near home.

Rapid transportation, rapid change

By the beginning of the 20th century, the next leap forward in the story of transportation had taken place. The first cars were on the road, and the first airplanes were in the air. Suddenly, the world seemed a smaller place, and the pace of change got faster. Cars became cheaper and better designed; aircraft grew in size and got faster; ocean liners became more luxurious and cargo vessels got bigger. In every area of transportation, engines were made more powerful and more efficient, and there were improvements in comfort and

Willys Jeep

safety. Today in the developed world, many families own at least one car, and regular air travel is a reality. In 1961 the Russians amazed the world by sending the first person into space.

By the end of the 1960s, men had walked on the Moon, and in the next decade unmanned space probes were sent out into the solar system. Nearer the ground, the supersonic jet, *Concorde*, had cut down the travel time between London and New York to only three hours.

Travel in the future

In the future, transportation on the ground and at sea may also become much swifter, with faster trains, cars, and ships on the drawing board. Governments and manufacturers are trying to make transportation more efficient so we use less of the world's precious resources as we travel. There are already exciting experimental boats and cars powered by the sun, and many scientists hope that the fuel cell, already used in some spacecraft, will one day provide quiet, efficient, low-

energy power for many other vehicles. Meanwhile, designers are always coming up with ways of making cars, trains, boats, and planes more streamlined, to cut down on drag and get more speed with less fuel. The resulting vehicles perform better, and often look great, too.

How to use this book

This book is divided into five easy-to-follow sections dealing with transportation on the road, in the water, in the air, and in space. Within each section, most of the pages contain a series of catalog-style entries on a range of craft and vehicles. Each entry contains the story of the vehicle and a fact box to see at-a-glance the speed and size, and the number of people carried. In addition, each section contains feature pages that deal with especially interesting topics, such as Formula One racing, high-speed trains, or developments in low-energy transportation. Finally, at the back of the book, you will find fact-packed lists on famous people, amazing transportation facts, what the technical terms mean, and a timeline of transportation history.

Skylab

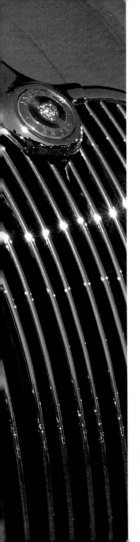

On Wheels

Long before the invention of the automobile, there was plenty of road transportation—chariots, stagecoaches, Hansom cabs, and other vehicles. Bumpy roads made long journeys uncomfortable, but they were possible.

When the automobile was invented at the end of the 19th century, some people tried to ban it, and control its speed so it did not frighten horses. Early laws even required someone to walk ahead of the car waving a red flag, although this was often hard to enforce. However, the car grew in popularity. In 1908 the first mass-produced car, the American Model T Ford, or "Tin Lizzie" opened up the prospect of cheap transportation for everyone. By 1922 there were 2 million Model Ts alone, and by the year 2000, 35 million cars were being produced each year.

Morris Cowley "Bullnose"

With his **Morris Cowley** and **Morris Oxford** "Bullnose" family cars, William Morris brought mass motoring to Britain in the 1920s. At that time there was also, and still is, a demand for luxury cars— Jaguar has been famous for producing luxury sports cars and sports sedans, like the MkII (left).

7

Who invented the wheel?

The first wheels were made about 3500 B.C. in Mesopotamia, the area between the Tigris and Euphrates rivers, in what is now Iraq. No one knows the names of the craftsmen who made these early wheels, but they probably got the idea from potters, who were using spinning wheels to make vessels out of clay. Like the potters' wheels, these early cartwheels were made of solid wood. Some 2,000 years later, fast two-wheeled chariots ran on spoked wheels. After another 2,000 years there were metal wheels, improved wheel bearings, and air-filled tires for a bump-free ride.

Primitive wheels were made of planks of wood held together with wooden pegs and mounted on axles. These **solid wheels** were used on carts to carry peat and on primitive chariots (*below*), and were very heavy to pull. Craftsmen from Mesopotamia (in modern day Iraq) removed some of the wood to make a wheel with two large holes, the forerunner of the spoked wheel.

Tires were first put onto wheels by the ancient Egyptians, who covered the rims of their wooden wheels with leather to protect them from wear. Solid rubber tires appeared in the 1840s, and in 1888 **John Boyd Dunlop** (*shown here*) equipped his son's bicycle with inflatable rubber tires. Today, most road vehicles have inflatable tires.

The **sleigh** (*above*) was in use before the wheel, and it still transports inhabitants of northern Siberia. The Inuits of northern Canada use the motorized **skidoo** (*right*), or snowmobile, to get over the ice.

Before he reinvented the home vacuum cleaner, James Dyson used a plastic ball as an alternative wheel to give his **Dyson ball barrow** a smooth ride over rocky or bumpy terrain. The ball is less likely to sink into soft earth than a traditional wheel, which makes it good for gardeners.

9

Before Engines

Once people discovered how to roll rather than slide things, transportation became much easier. By 3000 B.C., domesticated animals were harnessed to pull carts, the designs of which improved over the centuries. There were experiments using sails and even wind-up motors, but oxen were the most common.

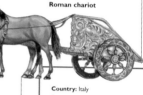

Roman chariot

Country: Italy
Date: c.200 B.C.
Size: 13¼ ft. (4.2 m) long
Body: wood
Top speed: 15 mph (24 km/h)
On board: 1 or 2

Oxen farm cart

Country: Europe
Date: 1100s A.D.
Size: 10 ft. (3 m) long
Body: wood
Top speed: 3 mph (5 km/h)
On board: 0

Oxen farm cart

After the invention of the wheel (see page 8), sledges were modified into simple carts. In the 1100s A.D., these carts were used for farm work with oxen to pull them. Each cart could carry much more produce at one time than ever before.

Roman chariot

Chariots were pulled by two, three, or four horses, and the one or two passengers used to stand. The Roman army used chariots to transport spear carriers and archers. Fighting chariots even had sharp blades attached to the wheels. Chariot racing was very popular.

Chinese wheelbarrow

Wheelbarrows were first used in China around 200 A.D. They were different from modern garden barrows because they had the load over the wheel rather than behind it, which made them easier to lift. Some barrows even had sails to help them move.

Chinese wheelbarrow

Country: China
Date: c.200 A.D.
Size: 5 ft. (1.5 m) long
Body: wood with fabric sail
Top speed: 2½ mph (4 km/h)
On board: 0

Country: Europe
Date: c.1600s A.D.
Size: 11 ft. (3.4 m) long
Body: wood
Top speed: 1¼ mph (2 km/h)
On board: 2

Treadmill carriage

Treadmill carriage

One of many attempts at replacing animals to pull carts was this self-propelled carriage. It was steered by rope, and power came from the man at the back "walking" on a tread wheel that made the rear axle turn. In fact, it would have been easier to push the vehicle. Obviously, it was a failure.

Hansom cab

Country: Britain
Date: 1834
Size: 6 ft. (1.8 m) long
Body: wooden body and wheels, with iron tires
Top speed: 6½ mph (10 km/h)
On board: 2 plus driver

Hansom cab

John Hansom invented this light and elegant two-wheeled cab. It was a common sight in Victorian London. The driver stood at the back and on top of the cab, and he could talk to his passengers through a trap door in the roof. There was a folding door at the front and a bench seat above the two wheels.

Concord stagecoach

By 1802, Americans could travel the 1,200 mi. (1,900 km) from Boston to Savannah in "stages" by different coaches. The best known stagecoach was the *Concord*, of which nearly 4,000 were made. They carried passengers inside with a driver and guard on top with the luggage. Leather springs made the ride more comfortable, with greater speed given by six horses.

Country: U.S.A.
Date: 1830
Size: 12 ft. (3.7 m) long
Body: wood with leather springs, metal strengthening
Top speed: 15 mph (24 km/h)
On board: 6 plus 2 crew

Concord stagecoach

Country: U.S.A.
Date: 1850s
Size: 12 ft. (3.7 m) long
Body: wood
Top speed: 3¼ mph (6 km/h)
On board: 2 or 3

Covered wagon

Canvas-covered wagons were the caravans or trailers of the 1850s. Some 55,000 pioneers used them to head west, often in groups called wagon trains. The wooden frames could carry several tons, and were usually hauled by oxen or mules— often in teams of six—and could only manage about 20 mi. (30 km) a day.

Covered wagon

11

Pedal Power

Most modern bicycles are still based on designs over 150 years old. The first pedal cycle was the *velocipe* of 1865, built by Michaux in France. It was very heavy, and the thick iron tires made the ride very bumpy, leading to the nickname "boneshaker." Today, some bikes are so light they can be lifted with just one finger.

Country: France
Date: 1816
Size: 6 ft. (1.8 m)
Body: iron frame and wheels, with leather seat
Propulsion: feet on ground

Penny-farthing

Dandy horse

Dandy horse

Also called the "hobby horse," this bicycle had two spoked wheels in line joined by a frame, just like a modern bike, but it had no pedals. Instead, the rider walked while sitting astride the machine to speeds of 9½ mph (15 km/h).

Country: Britain, U.S.A., France
Date: 1872
Size: 5 ft. (1.5 m)
Body: steel frame and spoked wheels, with leather saddle
Propulsion: pedals on front wheel

Penny-farthing

The earliest bicycles had the pedals working directly on the front wheels. This meant that a bigger wheel made the bike travel farther for each turn, so the wheels grew bigger (and the back wheel smaller) until some were 5 ft. (1.5 m) across. This was the ordinary bicycle of 1872, better known as the *penny-farthing* because it resembled two British coins of the day.

Country: Britain
Date: 1886
Size: 5¼ ft. (1.7 m)
Body: tubular steel frame with rubber tires and leather seat
Propulsion: chain drive from pedals

Raleigh Superbe

Touring bikes such as the *Raleigh Superbe* were made in the 1950s as the demand for cycles for leisure travelers and commuters increased. Its simple three-speed gear system made climbing hills easier, the chain had a cover to keep grease off clothes, and there were mudguards and lights.

Starley's Safety 1886

Raleigh Superbe

Country: Britain
Date: 1949
Size: 6 ft. (1.8 m)
Body: tubular steel frame with leather seat and steel mudguards
Propulsion: chain drive from pedals, with gears

Starley's Safety 1886

This bicycle looked very much like a modern bicycle with equal-sized wheels. It featured a rear wheel driven by a large chain wheel on the pedals, and a small chain wheel on the rear wheel giving it gears. The tires were solid rubber, and the bike shook a lot, but it made cycling much more popular, taking the place of the *penny-farthing*.

Marin Mount Vision

Country: U.S.A.
Date: 1999
Size: 5½ ft. (1.6 m)
Body: lightweight
aluminum frame with
full suspension
Propulsion: chain
drive with 21 gears

Marin Mount Vision

This lightweight mountain bike was the first with suspension on both front and rear wheels to win a major cross-country championship. The nobbly tires are tough and give extra grip on loose surfaces. The bike's tubing is made of aircraft-quality aluminum.

GTRZ 1000 Racer

Racing bikes have dropped handlebars so the rider can bend down for low wind resistance. They have thin, high-pressured tires and "derailleur" gears using a tight chain that can be moved from one size of sprocket (small, toothed wheel) to another, either at the pedals or at the wheel. Together, there can be as many as 21 gears.

Country: Britain
Date: 1992
Size: 6 ft. (1.8 m)
Body: lightweight carbon
composite frame and wheels
Propulsion: chain drive, no gears

GTZR 1000 Racer

Country: U.S.A.
Date: 1999
Size: 6 ft. (1.8 m)
Body: lightweight aluminum
frame with carbon fiber forks
Propulsion: chain drive from
pedals with 18 gears

Lotus Sport bike

Lotus Sport bike

Better known for its sports cars, Lotus came up with a very different-looking racing bike in 1992. Chris Boardman of Britain rode one to win a gold medal at the Barcelona Olympics. Instead of traditional steel tubing welded together, this bike was molded using stronger and lighter carbon fiber composite. New "tri-bar" handlebar designs gave the rider an ultra-low position.

What is a car?

The wheel was invented over 5,000 years ago, but the car has only been around for 100 years. In such a short time, this vehicle has changed the way we live and move around. How would we manage without this handy form of transportation that has developed from a basic horseless carriage to a high-tech road machine?

Sedan

Station wagon

Hatchback

Sports

Convertible

Compact

Off-road

Stretched

Mini van

Parts of a car

Nearly all cars have four wheels, and each one has a spring and damper to absorb the bumps. The engine is usually at the front and is usually mounted sideways. It drives the front wheels only. Car bodies are made of steel, aluminum, plastic, or fiberglass.

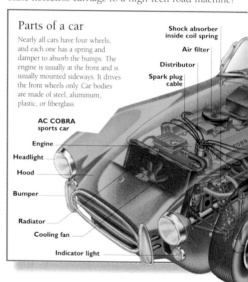

**AC COBRA
sports car**

Engine

Headlight

Hood

Bumper

Radiator

Cooling fan

Indicator light

**Shock absorber
inside coil spring**

Air filter

Distributor

**Spark plug
cable**

Car types

The cars (*left*) show the amazing variety of shapes and sizes available today—from seven-seater mini vans to two-seater sports convertibles. Compact cars are designed for the city, while off-road vehicles were made for the roughest tracks.

Tire types

All tires are round and black. Standard tires have grooves to clear away water, but off-road versions have deeper grooves to grip better in mud. Old tires were very narrow and had little grip.

High drag

Low drag

Aerodynamics (airflow)

Car designers and engineers use wind tunnels to check a car's aerodynamics. A ribbon of smoke is blasted along the tunnel, and this ribbon flows over the car showing if it has a smooth shape with low "drag," which means more speed for less fuel. Aerodynamic studies are also used to make cars stable on the road at high speed.

How engines work

Gasoline engines have cylinders with pistons going up and down inside them. The pistons are driven down by a mixture of gas and oil burning quickly above them. The up-and-down movement is turned in rotation by connecting rods linking the pistons to the crankshaft. The crankshaft is joined to the wheels of the car by the clutch and the transmission. The camshaft (controls) opens and closes the valves to let in the correct fuel and air mixture and to let the exhaust gases out of the cylinder.

Valves
Cylinder
Camshaft
Crankshaft
Piston

Front windshield
Trunk
Two-seater
Brake disk
Steering wheel
Steering column
Exhaust pipe

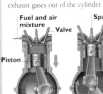

Early solid rubber
Early air-filled
Standard grooves
Racing (no grooves)

Fuel and air mixture
Valve
Spark plug
Exhaust
Piston

1.   2.   3.   4.

The four-stroke cycle

Most engines run on the four-stroke or Otto cycle. As a piston moves down the cylinder, a valve opens to allow the fuel and air mixture to be sucked in (1). As the piston starts to rise again, the valve closes and the mixture is compressed (2). Near the top of the piston stroke, a spark plug ignites the mixture, which burns quickly and expands to push the piston down again (3). Near the bottom once more, another valve opens to allow the rising piston to force the waste "exhaust" gas out (4). Then the cycle starts again.

15

The First Cars

In 1769 French army officer Nicholas Cugnot built the first self-propelled steam vehicle—a tractor to pull army guns, but it crashed into a wall. About 100 years later, Karl Benz and Gottlieb Daimler developed the first crude gas-engined buggies. These first cars were unreliable and could barely reach 9 mph (15 km/h). Nevertheless, the "horseless" carriage was overtaking the horse and carriage, and soon the first modern-looking cars appeared with engines mounted in the front.

La Mancelle

Country: France
Date: 1878
Size: 13 ft. (4 m) long
Body: wood and steel
Top speed: 6.5 mph (10 km/h)
On board: 6 plus firearm at rear

Benz "Motorwagen"

The first workable car, named after its inventor Karl Benz, was a three-wheeled vehicle with a tubular steel frame and an open wooden two-seater body. The single front wheel was steered by a tiller, while the two larger rear wheels were driven by chains. The gasoline engine was mounted horizontally at the back between the rear wheels.

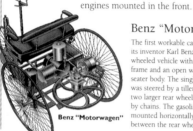

Benz "Motorwagen"

Country: Germany
Date: 1885/86
Size: 8 ft. (2.5 m) long
Body: wood and steel
Top speed: 8 mph (13 km/h)
On board: 2

Country: Germany
Date: 1893
Size: 8 ft. (2.5 m) long
Body: wood and steel
Top speed: 15 mph (25 km/h)
On board: 2

La Mancelle

Amédée Bollée's *La Mancelle* steamer set the style for cars to come. It featured a front-mounted engine driving the rear wheels, and a steering shaft, transmission and rods to swivel the wheels. Though not fast, *La Mancelle* ("The Girl from Le Mans") did knock down a horse.

Benz Viktoria

Benz Viktoria

The *Viktoria* was the first four-wheeler from Karl Benz, one of the most famous names in the automobile industry. It was also the first car to carry a model name and had an accurate steering system using a crude steering wheel rather than a tiller or lever. The *Viktoria* was also the first car to go into proper production. However, it still looked like a cart that had lost its horses.

Panhard-Levassor

Early French carmakers René Panhard and Emile Levassor designed a car that set the standard for other car-makers to follow: a front-mounted engine, the transmission in the middle, and rear-wheel drive.

Country: France
Date: 1894
Size: 8 ft. (2.5 m) long
Body: wood and steel
Top speed: 12½ mph (20 km/h)
On board: 4

Panhard-Levassor

Stanley Model 71

Country: U.S.A.
Date: 1910
Size: 11½ ft. (3.5 m) long
Body: steel and wood
Top speed: 55 mph (88 km/h)
On board: 4

Stanley Model 71

Steam power was still a serious rival to gasoline in the early days of automobiles. The American Stanley twins built successful mass-produced steam cars right into the 1920s. This 20-horsepower tourer had its boiler mounted under the hood and the engine at the back driving the rear wheels.

Renault Buggy

Louis, Marcel, and Fernand Renault founded one of the most famous French carmaking companies. Their first cars used de Dion engines, and this early model had a 1¾-horsepower engine under a half-rounded hood in the front driving the rear wheels. Renault also produced one of the first cars with a completely enclosed body.

Oldsmobile Curved Dash

Oldsmobile Curved Dash

Named after the shape of the footboard at the front, the *Curved Dash* was the world's first mass-produced car. A factory fire destroyed all the drawings, but the first model survived, and 4,000 copies were made at the Ransom E Olds factory in Lansing, Michigan, between 1901 and 1905. Hundreds of parts were made and assembled there to complete each car.

Country: U.S.A.
Date: 1901
Size: 8 ft. (2.5 m) long
Body: wood and steel
Top speed: 20 mph (32 km/h)
On board: 2

Renault Buggy

Country: France
Date: 1899
Size: 10 ft. (3 m) long
Body: wood and steel
Top speed: 12½ mph (20 km/h)
On board: 4

Luxury Cars

The bodies of the first cars were hand-built from the finest wood and hand-painted, with fully upholstered seats, carpets and curtains—reflecting the luxury of horse-drawn carriages before them. The 1920s saw the coachmaker's craft at its peak with royalty and movie stars demanding leather seats, walnut dashboards and even gold or silver plating. The luxury car market continues today with features such as multimedia consoles and space-age navigation systems.

Bugatti 41 Royale

Known as the "Golden Bug," the gigantic *Bugatti Royale* was so large that a *Mini* (see page 22) could be parked on its bonnet. Designed for monarchs, only six examples were sold. The engines later found use in high-speed French railcars.

Bugatti 41 Royale

Country: France
Date: 1926
Size: 22 ft. (6.7 m) long
Body: steel
Top speed: 100 mph (160 km/h)
On board: 6

Delage D8

Country: France
Date: 1930
Size: from 16 ft. (4.8 m) long
Body: steel
Top speed: 100 mph (160 km/h)
On board: 2 to 6 depending on body style

Delage D8

Louis Delage started building cars in 1906, and in 1912 he sold 1,000 vehicles. His cars were successful in the first international road races—one model won the Indianapolis "500" in 1914. The luxury tourer *D8* could manage 0–60 mph (0 to 100 km/h) in about 15 seconds, while the *D8SS* sports version averaged 112 mph (180 km/h) during 12 hours in trials.

Hispano-Suiza H6-B

Designed by Swiss engineer Mark Birkigt, this was the most technically advanced car in the world from 1919 to 1938. Hispano also made aircraft engines, and they developed a six-cylinder engine for this car as well as advanced four-wheel brakes.

Country: France
Date: 1919
Size: 16 ft. (4.8 m) long
Body: steel
Top speed: 85 mph (137 km/h)
On board: 2 to 6 depending on body style

Hispano-Suiza H6-B

Silver Ghost

Country: Britain
Date: from 1906
Size: from 15½ ft. (4.7 m) long
Body: steel
Top speed: 53 mph (85 km/h)
On board: 4

Silver Ghost

Rolls-Royce's elegant luxury car, the *40/50 hp* (hp for horsepower), was so quiet it earned the name "Silver Ghost." One model actually had silver-plated chromework, and this model was produced for 19 years with a variety of elegant bodies to suit individual owners.

Country: U.S.A.
Date: 1974
Size: 20 ft. (6 m) long
Body: steel
Top speed: 120 mph (192 km/h)
On board: 6

Lincoln Town Car

Mercedes Benz S-Class

With a sleeker body than before, this top-of-the-line sedan had just about every possible accessory, together with all kinds of electronic wizardry, such as rain-sensing windshield wipers and electric seats with built-in memory.

Mercedes Benz S-Class

Lincoln Town Car

Lincoln is still the Ford Motor Company's luxury American brand. It started as an independent company in the 1920s and was named after the founder's hero, President Lincoln. This 1970s *Town Car* had a distinctive coffin-shaped hood and retractable headlights. Its great size was typical of American sedans of the time, as was the "gas-guzzling" 7.5-liter V8 engine.

Country: Germany
Date: 1999
Size: 16½ ft. (5.1 m) long
Body: steel
Top speed: from 145 mph (232 km/h)
On board: 5

Country: Japan
Date: 1998
Size: 16¼ ft. (5 m) long
Body: steel
Top speed: 143 mph (230 km/h)
On board: 5

Lexus GS300

Lexus is the name the Japanese Toyota company uses for its luxury line of cars. The *GS300* has a powerful six-cylinder engine and a satellite navigation system that has voice instructions to guide the driver to his or her destination.

Lexus GS300

People Movers

The earliest cars could often seat four people, but the price was too high for the average family. It was only when Henry Ford put his famous *Model T* into mass (factory) production that family driving became a real possibility. Since then, this type of car, with plenty of seats and doors, has been the most popular, with many manufacturers competing hard to win sales. Today, mini vans have become very fashionable, particularly for larger families, but medium-sized sedans are as much in demand as ever.

Morris Cowley

William Morris left school at 15, repaired bicycles and cars, and bought a garage in Oxford, England. From 1913 to 1926 his *Cowley* was a rival to the American *Model T Ford*. Also called "bullnose" (because of the shape of the radiator), over 50,000 of these family cars were sold.

Model T Ford

Morris Cowley

Model T Ford

"Any color as long as it's black" was one of the sayings for which car-maker Henry Ford was famous. It applied to his *Model T Ford*, also known as the "Tin Lizzie" which introduced machine-made cars for the masses for the first time. Between 1908 and 1927, more than 15 million *Model Ts* were made. Such was the speed of production that there was no time to paint cars different colors at first.

Country: U.S.A.
Date: 1908
Size: from 1½ ft. (3.5 m) long
Body: steel
Top speed: 45 mph (72 km/h)
On board: 2 to 4 depending on body style

Country: Britain
Date: 1913
Size: 12 ft. (3.7 m) long
Body: steel
Top speed: 50 mph (80 km/h)
On board: 2 to 4 depending on body style

Volkswagen Beetle

This simple but innovative car, with its air-cooled engine, was designed by Dr. Ferdinand Porsche (see page 24) in 1936. He was responding to the German government's demand for a *volkswagen* ("people's car"). Although many thought it ugly, it became the best-selling car of all time.

Volkswagen Beetle

Country: Germany
Date: 1939
Size: 13 ft. (4 m) long
Body: steel
Top speed: 60 mph (100 km/h)
On board: 4

Country: U.S.A.
Date: 1958
Size: 18 ft. (5.5 m) long
Body: steel
Top speed: 100 mph
(160 km/h)
On board: 6

Rambler Ambassador

Country: France
Date: 1961
Size: 12 ft. (3.6 m) long
Body: steel
Top speed: 70 mph
(112 km/h)
On board: 4

Renault 4

Rambler Ambassador

Huge hoods, high tail fins, plenty of chrome-plated steel, and big, thirsty V8 engines were common in 1950s American family cars. It was a "glamour" look. The *Ambassador* had four doors but no fixed support between the side windows.

Renault 4

Renault President Pierre Dreyfus dreamed of a car for all types of people, what he called the "Blue Jeans Car," and the Renault 4 was the result. Rugged, basic, and inexpensive, it performed well on all types of terrain, and with five doors it provided compact family transport. Six million were sold.

Rover 75

Despite good press reviews, which can influence people's purchasing decisions, the 75 sold poorly. Rover got into trouble, and BMW, the German owners sold the company. The styling has a solid, old-fashioned look to lend a feeling of quality. Chrome trim and small windows are unusual in modern cars, but are part of a trend for "retro" (old style) designs.

Country: Britain
Date: 1999
Size: 15¾ ft. (4.8 m) long
Body: steel
Top speed: from 115 mph
(184 km/h) depending on engine
On board: 5

Country: U.S.A.
Date: 2000
Size: 15½ ft. (4.7 m) long
Body: steel
Top speed: 109 mph (175 km/h)
On board: up to 7

Rover 75

Chrysler Voyager

Chrysler Voyager

As a multipurpose vehicle, or mini-van, the Chrysler *Voyager* was intended to provide the space of a small minibus and the comfort of a luxury car. Features include chairs that swivel to face each other and sliding doors on each side to give ease of access.

Compact Cars

Small cars have small engines, use less fuel, and so are cheaper to run. Their size makes them ideal for maneuvering through busy city traffic and parking in tight spaces. In the 1950s three-wheeled, rear-engined "bubble cars" started the trend, but the arrival of the Fiat 500 and the *Mini* in the late 1950s paved the way for the boom in compact cars. Later models, such as Renault's 5 and Clio, and Volkswagen's *Polo* and *Golf* continued the compact cars' popularity.

Citroën 2CV

Citroën 2CV

"Four wheels under an umbrella" was the brief to the designer of the 2CV in the 1930s. The design also had to stand up to crossing a field without breaking a basket of eggs on board. The *Deux Chevaux* (two horses) or *2CV* had a tiny air-cooled engine, lift-off doors, fold-back roof, and removable hammock seats. By 1984, five million had been sold.

Country: France
Date: 1948
Size: from 12½ ft. (3.8 m) long
Body: steel
Top speed: from 35 mph (55 km/h)
On board: 4

Heinkel/Trojan 200

Zippy three-wheeler "bubble cars" were produced by famous German aircraft manufacturers such as Messerschmitt and Heinkel. This model was later manufactured in Britain as the *Trojan*. Powered by a small single-cylinder motorcycle engine, it had a single front door, but could still house two people in comfort. They continued into the 1960s, until the *Mini* put an end to this particular fashion.

Country: Germany, Britain
Date: 1956
Size: 7¾ ft. (2.4 m) long
Body: steel
Top speed: 55 mph (88 km/h)
On board: 2

Heinkel/Trojan 200

Austin Seven

One of the most famous British cars of all, the *Austin Seven* set a new style during its 16-year life. Sturdier than the fragile cycle-cars of the day, it was very affordable, with many versions from tiny two-seaters to graceful sedans.

Austin Seven

Country: Britain
Date: 1923
Size: 8¾ ft. (2.7 m) long
Body: steel
Top speed: 40 mph (64 km/h)
On board: 2 to 4 depending on body style

Mini

At a time when most cars had dull designs, Alec Issigonis's *Mini* was revolutionary. This tiny car had good interior space, thanks to an engine mounted across the frame driving the front wheels. In its *Mini-Cooper* form, it had great racing success.

Mini

Country: Britain
Date: 1959
Size: 10 ft. (3 m) long
Body: steel
Top speed: from 72 mph (115 km/h)
On board: 4

Fiat 500

Fiat 500

The *Nuove Cinquecento* or *500* was the first true four-seater mini-car. It replaced the 1930s two-seater *Topolino* ("Little Mouse"), the first car for many Italian families. The 500cc twin-cylinder engine was hidden behind the back seat, so the hood was for luggage. By the time this tiny machine gave way to the Fiat 126 in the 1970s, over 3 million had been sold.

Country: Italy
Date: 1957
Size: 9 ft. (2.7 m) long
Body: steel
Top speed: 60 mph (96 km/h)
On board: 2 to 4

Country: Europe
Date: 1996
Size: 11¾ ft. (3.6 m) long
Body: steel
Top speed: 96 mph (155 km/h)
On board: 4

Ford Ka

Ford Ka

Ford's smallest car had a very round body and large plastic moldings all around to give it an unmistakable design. It came with all kinds of gadgets, such as air conditioning and anti-lock brakes. The *Ka* was selected for exhibition at the New York Museum of Modern Art for its styling and shape.

Toyota Yaris

Toyota's baby hatchback was acclaimed as European Car of the Year 2000. An apparently new concept saw the designers figuring out what interior space was needed for comfort and then building the car around that. This gave a tall, yet compact car, with good seating for four.

Toyota Yaris

Country: Japan
Date: 1999
Size: 11¾ ft. (3.6 m) long
Body: steel
Top speed: 96 mph (154 km/h) depending on model
On board: 4

Sports Cars

Sports cars are designed to accelerate from 0–60 mph (0 to 100 km/h) in just a few seconds, and some can reach speeds of up to 185 mph (300 km/h). Even though such speeds are well over legal road limits, people love the thrill of handling such powerful machines, especially compared with family sedans which are heavier, slower, and less responsive to fast turning or accelerating. Typical sports cars are two-seaters.

BMW Z3

Country: Germany, U.S.A.
Date: 1997
Size: from 13¼ ft. (4 m) long
Body: steel
Top speed: up to 140 mph (224 km/h)
On board: 2

Country: France
Date: 1997
Size: 12½ ft. (3.8 m) long
Body: fiberglass
Top speed: 135 mph (214 km/h)
On board: 2

Renault Spider

The *Spider* is an ultra-light and very basic two-seater, with a fiberglass body and an aluminum chassis. It is unlike anything else Renault has made. Just behind the seats is the 2.0-liter engine which drives the rear wheels, and gives the *Spider* great stability when cornering.

BMW Z3

Built first in the U.S.A. for Americans, this little German sports car quickly became popular in Europe, too. It is a traditional sports car, with only two seats and a front 3.2-liter engine driving the rear wheels. The Z3 also comes with an electrically operated hood.

Renault Spider

Porsche 911

Country: Britain
Date: 1957
Size: from 14¼ ft. (4.3 m) long
Body: steel
Top speed: 149 mph (240 km/h)
On board: 2

Jaguar XK-SS

This was a road-going version of the Le Mans 24-hour racing cars, the 1950s *D-type* Jaguars. Only 16 cars were completed before fire destroyed the factory where they were built. Those few cars are very valuable today, and the curved design of the *XK-SS* was developed into the world-famous *E-type* Jaguar.

Country: Germany
Date: 1964
Size: from 12¼ ft. (4.3 m) long
Body: steel
Top speed: 181 mph (290 km/h) in turbo versions
On board: 2

Porsche 911

The *911* was first made in 1964 and continued until 1997 without changing its sleek, aerodynamic shape. All models had their air-cooled engines mounted behind the rear wheels, and they required care when cornering at speed.

Jaguar XK-SS

Jeep Wrangler

Country: U.S.A.
Date: 1998
Size: 12¾ ft. (3.9 m) long
Body: steel
Top speed: 92 mph (147 km/h)
On board: 4

Jeep Wrangler

This modern open top is fun and safe. It comes equipped with safety features such as airbags, all-steel doors and a skid plate under the fuel tank, and a transmission case to protect the underside of the vehicle. Four-wheel drive can be selected on the move if needed suddenly.

Toyota Land Cruiser

Launched as a basic but rugged all-terrain vehicle, the *Land Cruiser* has sold in vast numbers worldwide. Today, it is made in two luxury versions, the *Colorado* and the *Amazon*. There is an on-board compass, an inclinometer to tell you how steep a track is, and even an altitude display. This is a people carrier with the roadholding stability of a four-wheel drive.

Country: Japan
Date: 2000
Size: 14 ft. (4.3 m) long
Body: steel
Top speed: 100 mph (160 km/h)
On board: 8

Toyota Land Cruiser

Country: U.S.A.
Date: 2000
Size: 15¾ ft. (4.8 m) long
Body: steel
Top speed: 100 mph (160 km/h)
On board: 5

Ford Explorer

The *Explorer* is an old favorite in the U.S., and it is now a top-selling off-road vehicle in Europe, too. It features a big engine, selectable four-wheel drive, and automatic transmission (clutch and gearbox) to help it through tough terrain. It is also well equipped for family driving. Air conditioning, electric windows, mirrors, sliding roof and seats, cruise control, and even an electronic compass are some of the on-board items.

Ford Explorer

The race flags

Officials at race meetings still use flags to get messages to drivers, though most communications are electronic and the cars have radios.

 **Yellow flag** shows that there is danger ahead, such as an accident.

Blue flag shows that a faster car is coming up, usually to lap a driver.

Green flag shows that the track is clear, particularly after yellow flags.

Black flag with a car's number on it indicates that the car must stop.

Red flag shows that a race has been stopped.

White flag warns there is a slow-moving vehicle ahead (i.e., an ambulance).

Yellow and red flag warns that the track ahead is unusually slippery.

Checkered flag is waved at the finish line, when the winner passes.

Formula One Cars

Formula One cars are the fastest—reaching speeds of 200 mph (320 km/h)—and the drivers are the most skilled in the world. There is only room for one person, who sits in front of the engine. The wheels are uncovered, and the tires are very wide to grip the road well. Wings are used at the front and back to press the cars down and help them to go around corners fast. The wings give so much downward force at high speed that the cars could drive along a ceiling upside down without falling off.

The pit crew

A large team of people look after each car at a Grand Prix race. They work very fast during the race, changing four tires and filling the fuel tank in less than 10 seconds.

 Crash helmet

Flameproof protection suit

Protective clothing

Every driver wears a crash helmet to protect his head in a crash and a special suit to help prevent injury if a fire starts after an accident. The suit is made of several layers of special fireproof fabric.

Front wing or aerofoil

F1 CAR DESIGN

Racing cars

Racing and sports cars have changed a great deal since the early 1900s, when cars used to carry riding mechanics. Some early racers had huge engines, which made them very fast, but they were heavy and their tires were narrow, so the grip on corners was poor. The modern design, with the engine just behind the driver, and the car as low as 35 in. (90 cm) began in the 1960s.

1914

1930

1939

1950

1963

1970

Transmission

Engine

Rear wings or aerofoils for downward force

Rear tire

Air inlet

Cockpit

Bathtub chassis

Hockenheim

Racing circuits

Most of the circuits used for Grand Prix are specially built, but one of the oldest, in the Principality of Monaco, is on ordinary roads, with safety barriers put up for the race. Because this circuit is narrow and twisty, it is slow, but others, such as Hockenheim in Germany, have long straights that allow the cars to go very fast.

Monaco

Front wheel

Front suspension

29

Car Racing

Since the earliest days of automobiles there have been races: the French Grand Prix dates back to 1906. At that time, racing cars were huge machines capable of 90 mph (145 km/h). Today's race cars can comfortably reach 200 mph (320 km/h). But not all racing takes place on a race track. Rallying is almost like off-road racing, often on dirt tracks, where the driver relies on side spins to corner, the opposite of circuit racing, in which smooth-turning drivers are the quickest.

Zip Kart

Country: various
Date: 1992
Size: 6 ft. (1.8 m) long
Body: steel tube frame and seat
Top speed: 150 mph (240 km/h)
On board: 1

Ford Focus

Ford Focus

This rally version of a standard *Focus* has extra body strength and special suspension. The engine produces more than twice as much power as the standard road car, so it can go at very high speeds on rough windy tracks, often through thick forests. When they are rallying, the driver and his navigator talk to each other through an intercom in their helmets because it is so noisy.

Country: Britain
Date: 2000
Size: 13¾ ft. (4.2 m) long
Body: reinforced steel and carbon fiber
Top speed: 150 mph (240 km/h)
On board: 2

Zip Kart

This kart is light enough to be picked up by one person. It is made up of a tube frame with a seat, a steering wheel, pedals, and a small engine at the back. Because it is so small, it can "zip" around Grand Prix circuits at 150 mph (240 km/h), and its tiny tires are wide enough to allow the kart to go around corners very fast. Less powerful 25-mph (40-km/h) versions are popular at go-kart tracks.

Country: France
Date: 1999
Size: 15 ft. (4.6 m) long
Body: steel and composites
Top speed: 112 mph (180 km/h)
On board: 2

Schlesser Renault Buggy

Jean-Louis Schlesser's *Buggy* is strengthened and has special springs to tackle the tough desert surfaces on the 6,250 mi. (10,000 km) Paris-Dakar (Europe to Africa) Rally. The engine is from a Renault *Megane* road car, but it is highly modified for extra power.

Schlesser Renault Buggy

Audi/Le Mans

Audis are not usually associated with the famous Le Mans 24-hour race, but in 2000 an aerodynamic racing *Audi* won the event. It is built of lightweight materials, such as carbon fiber, and its engine, which sits behind the driver, can power it to speeds of well over 185 mph (300 km/h).

Audi/Le Mans

Country: Germany
Date: 2000
Size: 15 ft. (4.6 m) long
Body: carbon fiber
Top speed: 200 mph (320 km/h)
On board: 1 (officially 2)

Daf SRT-II

A turbocharged engine helps this racing truck accelerate fast enough to leave most sports cars behind. The cab is strengthened, leaving room for only a driver, and the truck is so light that more weight has to be put on to load it down.

Daf SRT-II

Country: Netherlands
Date: 1998
Size: 14¾ ft. (4.5 m)
Body: steel and lightweight composites
Top speed: 112 mph (180 km/h)
On board: 1

Ford Taurus

This Ford won the 1999 Daytona 500, which is the most famous NASCAR (National Association for Stock Car Auto Racing) event. It looks like a standard "stock" or sedan car that customers can buy, but in fact it has been altered to speed along banked oval circuits in some 30 races each year.

Country: U.S.A.
Date: 1999
Size: 16 ft. (5 m) long
Body: lightweight alloys
Top speed: 200 mph (340 km/h)
On board: 1

Ford Taurus

Reynard 961

Reynard 961

Like many Indy cars racing on the American road and oval race circuits, the Reynard is built in Britain. Though they look like Formula One racers (see pages 28–29), average lap speeds of these racing cars are 232 mph (373 km/h), and they run on alcohol fuel, not gasoline. A gear change takes 16 milliseconds, and a transmission copes in two hours with what a road car suffers in a lifetime.

Country: U.S.A.
Date: 1996
Size: 16 ft. (5 m) long
Body: lightweight composites
Top speed: 235 mph (376 km/h)
On board: 1

War Vehicles

The first military vehicles were the wheeled siege towers and battering rams used by the Assyrians of Asia in the 9th century B.C. Leonardo da Vinci drew a battle car in 1484, and in 1855 James Cowen invented an armed, wheeled, armored vehicle based on the steam tractor. World War I (1914–18), saw real mechanized warfare with the first steel-plated tanks. They moved on metal chains called tracks, and today are armed with powerful cannons on revolving turrets.

AC armored car

Country: Britain
Date: 1916
Size: 26½ ft. (8.1 m) long
Body: armored steel plates
Top speed: 3¾ mph (6 km/h)
On board: 8

AC armored car

This gunless armored car, made by AC, was one of the first produced. It had an ordinary car frame, with thick steel bodywork to protect the crew. The driver looked ahead through a small slit in the front, and even the radiator had armored doors. However, the wheels could easily be damaged, and the tires punctured in action.

Country: Britain
Date: 1914
Size: 12 ft. (3.7 m) long
Body: heavy steel
Top speed: 31 mph (50 km/h)
On board: 6

Vickers tank

Tanks were first made with caterpillar tracks to cross mud, trenches, and barbed wire during World War I. They were called "tanks" to conceal their real purpose from the enemy. The "male" *Vickers* had cannons on the side, and the "female" had machine guns. Their first battle was the Somme in 1916. Inside they were very hot, noisy, and uncomfortable.

Country: Germany
Date: 1940
Size: 12½ ft. (3.8 m) long
Body: steel
Top speed: 56 mph (90 km/h)
On board: 4

Kubelwagen

DUKW

DUKWs were nicknamed "Ducks" because they could travel over water from ship to shore at 6¼ mph (10 km/h). All the wheels steered, and helped the rudder in water. About 1,000 *DUKWs* took part in the invasion of Sicily (1943).

DUKW

Country: U.S.A.
Date: 1943
Size: 20 ft. (6 m) long
Body: mainly steel
Top speed: 50 mph (80 km/h) on land
On board: 25 to 30

Kubelwagen

The *Kubelwagen* was the German army's version of the VW *Beetle* (see page 20). It was designed by Dr. Porsche, and during World War II (1939–45), more than 50,000 were built. It did not have four-wheel drive, like the *Jeep* (see page 26), but with very simple mechanical parts, it was reliable. It was used to carry soldiers in battle areas, and there was even an amphibious version called the *Schwimmwagen*.

White M3A1 Scout Car

This was a popular command vehicle. It had four-wheel drive to cope with any terrain. Though it was armored and carried a machine gun, passengers were still exposed to enemy fire. Some were used as ambulances or to carry mechanics.

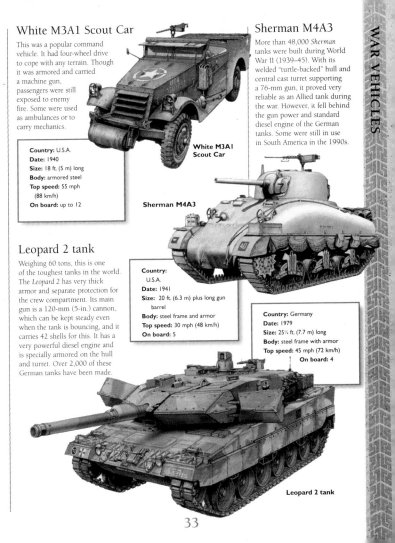

White M3A1 Scout Car

Country: U.S.A.
Date: 1940
Size: 18 ft. (5 m) long
Body: armored steel
Top speed: 55 mph (88 km/h)
On board: up to 12

Sherman M4A3

More than 48,000 *Sherman* tanks were built during World War II (1939–45). With its welded "turtle-backed" hull and central cast turret supporting a 76-mm gun, it proved very reliable as an Allied tank during the war. However, it fell behind the gun power and standard diesel engine of the German tanks. Some were still in use in South America in the 1990s.

Sherman M4A3

Country: U.S.A.
Date: 1941
Size: 20 ft. (6.3 m) plus long gun barrel
Body: steel frame and armor
Top speed: 30 mph (48 km/h)
On board: 5

Leopard 2 tank

Weighing 60 tons, this is one of the toughest tanks in the world. The *Leopard 2* has very thick armor and separate protection for the crew compartment. Its main gun is a 120-mm (5-in.) cannon, which can be kept steady even when the tank is bouncing, and it carries 42 shells for this. It has a very powerful diesel engine and is specially armored on the hull and turret. Over 2,000 of these German tanks have been made.

Country: Germany
Date: 1979
Size: 25¼ ft. (7.7 m) long
Body: steel frame with armor
Top speed: 45 mph (72 km/h)
On board: 4

Leopard 2 tank

Emergency Vehicles

We often see brightly marked police cars, ambulances, pick-up trucks, and fire engines with lights flashing or sirens wailing, hurrying through traffic. So it is hard to imagine that the earliest ambulances and fire engines were pulled by horses or people. A modern fire truck can carry 1,200 gallons (4,500 liters) of water and 1,500 ft. (450 m) of hose.

Willeme 5471

This aircraft recovery truck was built on a standard Willeme chassis (frame), but was specially adapted to recover aircraft that had broken down. It had 12 wheels on four axles so it could carry loads of up to 150 tons. A massive crane on the back was used to lift the aircraft, and the front of the truck had to be very heavy to make sure that it did not tip up.

Country: France
Date: 1956
Size: 35 ft. (10.7 m) long
Body: steel frame and cab
Top speed: 37½ mph (60 km/h)
On board: 2

Willeme 5471

Merryweather fire appliance

This fire engine had one of the early turntable ladders, which could be raised automatically to reach tall buildings quickly. The pump was driven by the truck's engine and could push water through its hoses up to a height of 130 ft. (40 m).

Merryweather fire appliance

Country: Britain
Date: 1922
Size: 24¼ ft. (7.4 m) long, plus ladder
Body: steel frame and cab
Top speed: 35 mph (56 km/h)
On board: 4

Country: U.S.A.
Date: 1989
Size: approx. 158 ft. (48 m)
Body: steel and aluminum
Top speed: 105 mph (65 km/h)
On board: 6

U.S. fire truck

This truck is very big, and it has all kinds of equipment on board. Its ladder has a platform on top and can go as high as a seven-story building. It can also rotate 360°, and the platform has two water cannons that can squirt about 1,500 gallons (5,600 liters) of water a minute on a fire. Outrigger legs on the side of the truck keep it steady when the platform is being used, and the truck has many spotlights and floodlights.

NYPD Impala

Country: U.S.A.	
Date: 2000	
Size: 16¾ ft. (5.1 m) long	
Body: steel	
Top speed: 124 mph (198 km/h)	
On board: 6	

NYPD Impala

The NYPD (New York Police Department) version of the Chevrolet *Impala* has a lot of special equipment. The engine is bigger and more powerful, the brakes are large, and the springs are tough. The roof lights and siren make sure that people know the police are coming. On the front are push bars that let the police move or stop other cars without damage to their car.

Country: Yugoslavia	
Date: 1975	
Size: 20¼ ft. (6.2 m) long	
Body: armored steel and glass	
Top speed: possibly 55 mph (90 km/h)	
On board: possibly 2 to 4	

FAP riot control

Specially designed to deal with rioting crowds, this van has four-wheel drive for rough or slippery ground and extremely tough bodywork. The exposed glass is armored, and the headlights have grills over them. What looks like a gun on the top is a water cannon, powerful enough to knock over and push back rioters. It is supplied from a big water tank inside the van.

FAP riot control

U.S. fire truck

U.S. wrecker

This piece of equipment took well over a year to complete, and is designed for towing and heavy duty recovery. The truck was made separately from the wrecker body. The wrecker body was built in Texas and mounted onto the stretched-out frame of the truck, which came from another part of the country. It is used for towing heavy vehicles.

U.S. wrecker

Country: U.S.A.	
Date: 1997	
Size: 39½ ft. (12 m) long	
Body: steel	
Top speed: approx. 56 mph (90 km/h)	
On board: 1, sometimes 2	

Trucks

The earliest trucks used gasoline engines or steam power, but in the 1920s the German Benz Company introduced diesel-powered trucks. Diesel engines were more powerful and meant trucks could travel farther on a single tank of fuel. Modern trucks are either "rigid" (having a single and straight chassis frame), or "jointed" with two parts: a tractor unit that carries the engine, cab, driving wheels, and a detachable trailer.

De Dion Bouton

Vabis 1½-ton truck

De Dion Bouton

Even in the early 1920s, some trucks were purpose-built to perform special tasks. This *De Dion Bouton* road-sweeper had a brush that turned as the truck moved and collected roadside trash. The dirt was then sucked into the bag on the back of the truck. The rest of the truck was old-fashioned, with open cabin sides and cart-type wheels.

Country: France
Date: 1922
Size: 16½ ft. (5 m) long
Body: wood and steel
Top speed: 20 mph (32 km/h)
On board: 2

Scammel Scarab

The *Scarab* could turn around in small spaces, because of a clever pivot between the cab and the trailer, the pointed nose, and the single front wheel. It was ideal for stations, where one tractor could handle several trailers.

Country: Britain
Date: 1949
Size: 29½ ft. (9 m) long
Body: steel (later fiberglass cab)
Top speed: 30 mph (48 km/h)
On board: 2

Scammel Scarab

Vabis 1½-ton truck

One of the first Swedish trucks, this *Vabis* had a simple platform on a steel girder frame. The tiny engine at the front drove the back wheels. There were springs, but the ride was not comfortable for the exposed driver.

Country: Sweden
Date: 1903
Size: 15 ft. (4½ m) long
Body: wood and steel with wooden wheels and steel tires
Top speed: 12½ mph (20 km/h)
On board: 2

CAT 621E scraper

These huge machines are often seen where big new roads are being built. Even the tires are taller than a person. These machines can scrape up to 13 in. (33 cm) of earth at a time to level the surface, and carry 22 tons of soil. The scraper is on a swiveling link to the tractor at the front, and both parts have a powerful diesel engine.

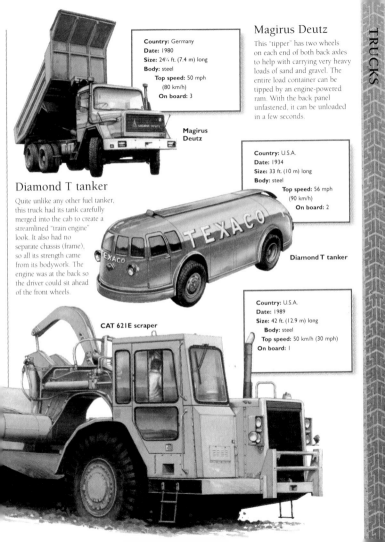

Magirus Deutz

This "tipper" has two wheels on each end of both back axles to help with carrying very heavy loads of sand and gravel. The entire load container can be tipped by an engine-powered ram. With the back panel unfastened, it can be unloaded in a few seconds.

Country: Germany
Date: 1980
Size: 24¼ ft. (7.4 m) long
Body: steel
  Top speed: 50 mph
    (80 km/h)
  On board: 3

Magirus Deutz

Diamond T tanker

Quite unlike any other fuel tanker, this truck had its tank carefully merged into the cab to create a streamlined "train engine" look. It also had no separate chassis (frame), so all its strength came from its bodywork. The engine was at the back so the driver could sit ahead of the front wheels.

Country: U.S.A.
Date: 1934
Size: 33 ft. (10 m) long
Body: steel
  Top speed: 56 mph
    (90 km/h)
    On board: 2

Diamond T tanker

CAT 621E scraper

Country: U.S.A.
Date: 1989
Size: 42 ft. (12.9 m) long
  Body: steel
  Top speed: 50 km/h (30 mph)
On board: 1

Buses

Some of the earliest buses were double-decker horse-drawn trams that ran through the streets on rails (see page 94). Motor-powered buses and trolleys appeared in the early 1900s. Most buses today run on their own engines, while trolleys are powered by electricity from overhead cables. Long-distance buses come with individual lighting, air controls, reclining seats, and are equipped with restrooms.

Germain open top

Bean single deck

Country: Belgium
Date: 1904
Size: 24 ft. (7 m) long
Body: wood and steel
Top speed: 20 mph (32 km/h)
On board: 32

Bean single deck

By today's standards, the *Bean's* engine was not powerful, and it took up a lot of room. With the driver and the door behind him, there was even less room for passengers. If the engine stopped, the driver might have to resort to restarting the bus by winding the handle hanging from the front.

Sunbeam trolley bus

Trolley buses have electric motors. They pick up electricity through "trollers" (arms) on the roof that run along overhead wires. They do not run on rails as trams do. On this double-decker version, the stairs to the top deck were at the back, and a conductor collected the fares while on the move. Sometimes, the arms would come off the wires and the driver would use a special long pole to push them back up.

Germain open top

Early buses, like this *Germain*, one, which was used in London, had its driver sitting on the hood to leave as much room as possible for passengers. An outside staircase led to the roof. People would have a good view from there, but would get wet if it rained. The ride was slow and bumpy, and the buses often broke down.

Country: Britain
Date: 1930
Size: 19½ ft. (6 m) long
Body: aluminum and wood
Top speed: 46¾ mph (75 km/h)
On board: 18

Country: Britain
Date: 1946
Size: 32¾ ft. (10 m) long
Body: steel
Top speed: 40 mph (64 km/h)
On board: 66

Sunbeam trolley bus

MCI courier

38

Berliet PCM bus

Berliet PCM bus

Although this French bus looks modern, it is more than 30 years old. It has doors at the front and the back, operated by the driver, so passengers can enter and leave without crowding. There is plenty of room for standing as well as sitting, with handrails to hold onto. The layout in which the driver sits alongside the engine is called forward control.

Country: France
Date: 1968
Size: 32¼ ft. (10 m) long
Body: steel and fiberglass
Top speed: 62 mph (100 km/h)
On board: 40

AmTran school bus

American school buses are made by many different companies, but they are always yellow and easy to spot. This one has a high floor with low doors for ease of access. Multiple mirrors allow the driver to make sure it is safe to drive off, and flashing lights on the top warn other drivers.

AmTran school bus

Country: U.S.A., Canada
Date: 1948
Size: 34½ ft. (10.5 m) long
Body: wood and steel
Top speed: 53 mph (85 km/h)
On board: 33

Country: U.S.A.
Date: 1999
Size: 31¼ ft. (9.5 m) long
Body: welded steel
Top speed: 65 mph (105 km/h)
On board: 54

MCI courier

This single-decker was the standard intercity passenger bus in the U.S. and Canada in the late 1940s and early 1950s. The American Greyhound line covers vast distances, so comfort is important. This was one of the first buses to have reclining seats. The high floor meant that passengers had a good view and that luggage could be stowed in a compartment below.

Motorcycles

Motorcycles are two-wheeled vehicles with engines, which a driver straddles as if on a bicycle. Some have a sidecar attached on a third wheel. Mopeds are low-powered motorcycles equipped with pedals to power the engine. Motorcycles also compete in road and cross-country (motocross) racing.

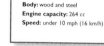

Daimler Einspur

Country: Germany
Date: 1885
Size: 5 ft. (1.5 m)
Body: wood and steel
Engine capacity: 264 cc
Speed: under 10 mph (16 km/h)

Henderson 7hp

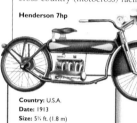

Henderson 7hp

American motorcycles developed as powerful tourers for the country's big roads. This model featured a powerful four-cylinder engine that was unusual for the time, in a very long frame. The machine was hard to control in tight turns. On the highway, however, it could cruise at over 50 mph (80 km/h).

Country: U.S.A.
Date: 1913
Size: 5¾ ft. (1.8 m)
Body: steel
Engine capacity: 1301 cc
Speed: 55 mph (88 km/h)

Daimler Einspur

The Daimler *Einspur* ("single track") may be the first true motorcycle, even though it had extra wheels to keep it stable and a seat that looked as if it had just been taken off a horse. A tall single-cylinder gas engine produced just half a horsepower.

Electra-Glide

Harley-Davidson was founded in 1903. The most famous model the company ever produced is the 1960s *Electra-Glide*, which is still in production, little altered from the original. It is popular with many police forces. The heart of the Glide is a big V-twin engine that produces a distinctive "potato-potato" noise.

Country: U.S.A.
Date: 1965
Size: 6½ ft. (2 m)
Body: steel
Engine capacity: 1207 cc
Speed: 95 mph (153 km/h)

Electra-Glide

Country: Italy
Date: 1963
Size: 5½ ft. (1.7 m)
Body: steel frame and panels
Engine capacity: 159 cc
Speed: 60 mph (96 km/h)

Vespa GS1 60

Vespa GS1 60

The *Vespa* (Italian for wasp) is a scooter—a motorcycle with a little engine mounted around the back wheel so the rider sits upright with feet together on a platform. It has a "step-through" frame; most controls (except the rear brake) are sited on the handlebars; and the engine is powerful enough to allow it to zip in and out of traffic.

Honda CB750

With a quiet and revolutionary four-cylinder engine (other bikes had just one or two cylinders), this was the first long-distance touring superbike. When bikes were still thought of as oily and unreliable, the electric-start engine was said to be "sewing-machine-smooth."

Honda CB750

Ducati 750SS

Country: Japan
Date: 1969
Size: 6½ ft. (2 m)
Body: steel
Engine capacity: 736 cc
Speed: 120 mph (193 km/h)

Country: Italy
Date: 1972
Size: 7 ft. (2.1 m)
Body: steel
Engine capacity: 748 cc
Speed: 126 mph (203 km/h)

Ducati 750SS

Capable of going over 124 mph (200 km/h), this *Ducati* model was a racing motorcycle for the road. It was also the forerunner of the famous red racers that dominated superbike racing in the 1990s. It had few comforts or frills for the road traveler, and was much more at home screeching at high speeds on the race tracks. Its engine was powerful, but the *Ducati* was also renowned for its fine handling and roadholding.

BMW C1

BMW C1

Perhaps the ultimate commuter vehicle, the BMW *C1* runs like a scooter (low-powered engine and low-slung frame with two small wheels). However, a roof, a windshield (and wiper), side protection bars, and twin seat belts have been added for extra safety.

Country: Germany
Date: 2000
Size: 6½ ft. (2 m)
Body: aluminum frame, plastic body
Engine capacity: 125 cc
Speed: 62 mph (100 km/h)

Mean Machines

There are some wheeled vehicles that stand out from the crowd. They are bigger, heavier, taller, longer, or faster than anything else. Some may have been "customized"—like hot-rod cars "sunk" low and equipped with extra-wide wheels and a powerful racing-tuned engine, or "stretched limos" with extra chassis and wheels to allow passengers to stretch out and enjoy television, a refrigerator, and a bar. Some are built for sport, others to carry important people safely with bullet- and bomb-proofing, and some to beat a speed or endurance record.

Bigfoot

Bigfoot began as a pick-up truck with big tires and suspension for car crushing displays at fairs. The tires are over 6 ft. (1.8 m) high. *Bigfoots* have powerful engines and lightweight bodies to set long jump records of over 200 ft. (62 m).

Bigfoot

Country: U.S.A.
Date: 1976
Size: 18 ft. (5.5 m) long
Body: alloys on a tubular frame
Top speed: 65½ mph (100 km/h)
On board: 2

AEC Mammoth Major

This 1960s "road-train" was specially built in Australia by the British AEC company. It could carry 100 tons of goods at a time across the vast Australian outback (where there are no railroads). Throwing up clouds of dust, it resembled a fast-moving crocodile in the sand.

AEC Mammoth Major

Country: Australia
Date: 1960
Size: 148 ft. (45 m) long with 3 trailers
Body: steel and alloys
Top speed: 55 mph (88 km/h)
On board: 3

Thrust SSC

This was the first car to break the sound barrier, at Black Rock Desert, Nevada, in October 1997. Driven by Andy Green, it took just 4.67 seconds to pass through the measured mile. At the record speed, the big aluminum wheels rotate 8,500 times a minute, and the parachutes released to slow down the vehicle give 10 tons of braking force.

Thrust SSC

Country: UK
Date: 1997
Size: 47¼ ft. (14.6 m) long
Body: steel frame, aluminum panels
Top speed: 763 mph (1,221 km/h)
On board: 1

Dragster

This dragster's huge engine is tuned to produce 6,000 horsepower for the four seconds it takes to pass through a measured mile. The front steering wheels are tiny, but the back tires are huge because they have to drive the dragster. The driver sits just behind the engine, which is cooled by ice and runs on an alcohol-based fuel.

Dragster

Country: U.S.A.
Date: 2000
Size: 19¾ ft. (6 m) long
Body: steel frame, some composite paneling
Top speed: 200 mph (320 km/h)
On board: 1

Peterbilt truck

With their chrome exhaust stacks pointing to the sky, such huge "long-nosed" trucks haul loads of more than 40 tons across North America. These massive transporters are built to travel several million miles in their lifetime.

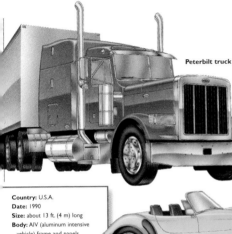

Peterbilt truck

Country: U.S.A.
Date: 1990s
Size: 40 ft. (12.2 m) long
Body: steel frame with aluminum cab
Top speed: 60 mph (96 km/h)
On board: 2 or 3

Country: U.S.A.
Date: 1990
Size: about 13 ft. (4 m) long
Body: AIV (aluminum intensive vehicle) frame and panels
Top speed: 143 mph (230 km/h)
On board: 2

Panoz AIV roadster

Panoz AIV Roadster

Looking like a 1950s hot rod, the *Panoz* has a powerful V8 engine delivering 305 horsepower. It can go from 0–60 mph (0 to 100 km/h) in 4.6 seconds. Each car takes 350 hours to hand build, and many of the parts are developed from racing cars.

Country: U.S.A.
Date: 1982
Size: 15 ft. (4.6 m) long
Body: steel and alloys
Top speed: 80 mph (128 km/h)
On board: up to 10

Hummer HMMWV

The *Hummer* was designed for the U.S. Army as a go-anywhere vehicle. The initials HMMWV stand for High Mobility Multi-Purpose Wheeled Vehicle, sometimes shortened to the name *Humvee*. Today it is very popular for civilian use. With four-wheel drive, it can climb up incredibly steep hills at 7 mph (11 km/h) and can go through up to 5 ft. (1.5 m) of water. It can do 0–50 mph (0 to 80 km/h) in 14 seconds. Customized versions include one with caterpillar tracks.

Hummer HMMWV

On Water

Boats and ships are the most varied of all forms of transportation, ranging from tiny dinghies only a few feet long to vast supertankers that take more than five minutes to walk around. From warships to windsurfers, there are vessels for virtually any task.

In the Stone Age, the earliest boat was a canoe hollowed out of a log. Then came oars and sails followed by steam and gasoline engines. Today, wave-piercing water jets and solar power move ships. The water speed record is now a staggering 317 mph (511 km/h).

Luxury liners (*left*) take vacation passengers to exotic ports around the world. Such vessels have never been more popular. Cunard's *Queen Mary 2*, for example, being launched in 2003, will carry 2,800 passengers at 34 mph (55 km/h), driven by environmentally friendly gas/turbine diesel power. It will be five times longer than Cunard's first steamship, *Britannia* (see page 57).

Dragonfly

Square sail

What is a ship?

Any large vessel that floats on the water can be called a ship. Smaller craft are called boats, and sailors often say that if a vessel is big enough to carry a boat, then that vessel is a ship. Every ship has a body called a hull, which in ancient times was made of wood, but is now more likely to be metal or fiberglass. Ships also have some means of propulsion, such as sails or an engine. They have been around for well over 10,000 years, and are used as warships, pleasure craft, and to carry cargo or passengers.

Lateen sail

Settee sail

Gaff sail

Lug sail

Sprit sail

Yard arms

Mast

Rudder

Stern

Hull

Anchor

Bowsprit

Bow

CLIPPER TYPE SAILING SHIP

Types of sail

There are dozens of types of sail. Western oceangoing ships most commonly used square sails which, in a fully rigged ship, could set three or more to a mast. Triangular sails, such as lateen sails or settees, are still favored in the Arab world.

Parts of a sailing ship

There are several vertical masts, with other timbers, such as horizontal yard arms, to support the sails. The bow (front) is often pointed, to cut smoothly through the water; the rudder which is used for steering, is at the stern (rear).

The weight of the boat displaces the water

The displaced water now equals the weight of the boat, and the boat floats

How a ship floats

A solid object sinks because it weighs more than the amount of water it displaces. All ships are hollow and therefore very light for their size. They only settle into the water until the amount that they displace equals their own total weight. The pressure of the water from below supports the rest of the ship above the surface.

Propulsion

Ships used to have sails or oars, but modern ships usually have an engine. This drives a number of propellers, which push the craft through the water. The first propellers had twin blades, but three- or four-bladed propellers are more efficient and powerful.

Hovercraft

Instead of floating, a hovercraft hovers on a cushion of air just above the surface of the water, or a swamp (or dry land). It has huge fans to create the air cushion, which is held in place by a rubber membrane called a skirt that stretches all around the hull.

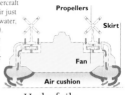

Hydrofoils

One thing that slows ships down is the force, called drag, created by the hull in the water. Hydrofoils get around this problem by raising their hull out of the water on special struts, called foils. Hydrofoils sit in the water like normal craft, but as they gather speed, the foils come into play, lifting up the hulls. This means that these craft can go much faster than standard vessels of the same power.

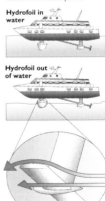

Hydrofoil in water

Hydrofoil out of water

At speed the foil lifts the hull out of the water

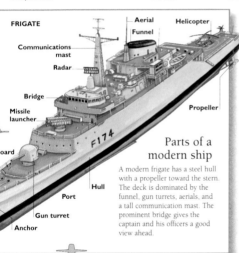

FRIGATE

Aerial

Helicopter

Funnel

Communications mast

Radar

Bridge

Missile launcher

Propeller

board

F174

Hull

Port

Gun turret

Anchor

Parts of a modern ship

A modern frigate has a steel hull with a propeller toward the stern. The deck is dominated by the funnel, gun turrets, aerials, and a tall communication mast. The prominent bridge gives the captain and his officers a good view ahead.

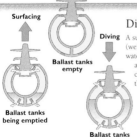

Surfacing

Ballast tanks empty

Ballast tanks being emptied

Diving

Ballast tanks filling up

Diving a submarine

A submarine contains large ballast (weight) tanks (heavily weighted with water): these can be filled or emptied as the vessel moves. When the captain wants to dive, he orders the tanks to be filled with water. This increases the weight and density of the submarine, which makes the vessel sink. To rise back to the surface, the water is pumped out from the tanks.

47

On the Water

Many of the first boats, including the North American kayak and the Polynesian outrigger, were so well crafted that similar boats are still used to transport people and goods 5,000 years later. When people first began to build boats, some chopped down tree trunks to make rafts or canoes, while others chose thin branches and animal skins to make frame boats. Ancient sailing vessels like dhows and junks are still made today and sail in the Arabian and China seas.

Coracle

Country: Ireland, Wales
Date: from pre-history
Size: 6½ ft. (2 m) long
Construction: hide on wicker framework
Speed: about 3½ mph (6 km/h)
On board: 1

Dugout canoe

Dugout canoe

The canoe was probably the first type of boat to be made. It consists of a tree trunk shaped and hollowed out in the middle to make a place where people could sit and paddle. Early people used simple stone axes to carve the wood to get the best hull shape. They used fire to hollow out the middle.

Country: worldwide
Date: from pre-history
Size: 10 ft. (3 m) long
Construction: wood
Speed: about 3½ to 7 mph (6 to 11 km/h)
On board: 2

Inuit kayak

Country: Canada
Date: from pre-history
Size: 18 ft. (5.5 m) long
Construction: seal skin on wood or bone frame
Speed: about 3½ to 7 mph (6 to 11 km/h)
On board: 1

Inuit kayak

For thousands of years the Inuit (Eskimo people of North America and Greenland) have built kayaks—long, narrow boats made of a wood or whalebone framework covered with skins. Kayaks are used for hunting and fishing, and their light weight makes them easy to carry. Their design makes them easy to return quickly to their upright position if they capsize.

Coracle

Shaped so it can be carried on the back, the coracle is an early lightweight boat. The design drawback is that it is not very stable in the water. The user needs to be experienced to keep it under control using only a simple wooden spadelike paddle. Like the kayak and similar portable boats, it is still used, mainly for fishing.

Wooden raft

The most basic water craft of all is the wooden raft. It is pushed along with a pole and is made of several logs lashed together with vines, twine, or some other binding material. Early raft-builders realized that their craft worked better if the logs had pointed ends, or if the entire raft front had a pointed shape.

Country: worldwide
Date: from pre-history
Size: 6½ ft. (2 m) long
Construction: wood
Speed: about 3½ to 7 mph (6 to 11 km/h)
On board: 1 or more

Wooden raft

Pacific outrigger

This type of boat was built by the sailors of the Pacific islands. The outriggers gave the craft great stability on the Pacific surf, in spite of the narrow hull. This type of hull with its large sail could travel very fast, and early navigators covered thousands of miles in boats like these. The modern day catamaran looks like this.

Chinese junk

Pacific outrigger

Country: China
Date: 9th century
Size: 20 to 250 ft. (6 to 137 m)
Construction: wood
Sail: hemp or matting with bamboo battens
On board: 1 to 250

Country: Polynesia, Micronesia
Date: from pre-history
Size: 30 ft. (9 m) long
Construction: tree bark, strips of wood
Sail: cotton or matting
On board: 1 or more

Arab dhow

With their sleek wooden hulls, flat sterns, and lateen (triangular) sails, the dhows of the Arab world are easy to recognize. They have one or two masts, and the lateen rig is especially good for sailing with winds from the side. They are used in the Red Sea, Indian Ocean, and Persian Gulf. Some dhows now have diesel engines.

Chinese junk

The junk is the traditional Chinese sailing ship that evolved in medieval times. The hull is made differently from that of a Western ship. Instead of getting its strength from a keel, the hull is divided by bulkheads (wooden partitions) that make the structure rigid. The sails are made of narrow strips of cloth held onto bamboo poles.

Arab dhow

Country: Red Sea, Persian Gulf
Date: from the 9th century
Size: 131 ft. (40 m)
Construction: wood
Sail: cotton or flax
On board: 18

Oars and Sails

All early civilizations depended on sea and river transportation. The ancient Egyptians traveled up and down the River Nile. The Greeks and Romans sailed all around the Mediterranean, relying on ships for both trade and war. These civilizations built the first sailing ships and used rows of oarsmen to propel a ship steadily and quickly over short distances. In addition, the Romans improved the steering oar, making their ships easier to move in battle.

Egyptian reed boat

Bundles of reeds were tied together with twine to make this early fishing boat. The papyrus reed, also used to make a paperlike writing material, was ideal for the job. It was light, easy to work, and was plentiful by the banks of the Nile.

Egyptian reed boat

Country: Egypt
Date: c.3000 B.C.
Size: 20 ft. (6 m) long
Construction: papyrus reeds
Sail material: flax (linen)
On board: 4 or 5

Egyptian wooden boat

Egyptian wooden boat

Among the world's first sailing vessels was this Egyptian wooden-hulled, single-masted, and square-sail boat. The rich could use them to travel along the Nile. A steersman controlled the boat with a large oar at the rear, and there were also long poles that the crew could use to push the vessel off sand banks. Larger versions were used to carry cattle and other cargo.

Country: Egypt
Date: c.2000 B.C.
Size: 39 ft. (12 m) long
Construction: cedar wood
Sail material: flax (linen)
On board: 10

Phoenician trader

The sea-trading Phoenicians built broad and deep-framed ships to carry cargoes of cloth and glassware around the Mediterranean. Their ships could have sails, oars, or both. Their wooden construction was very sturdy, and these vessels voyaged as far as Cornwall and Ireland.

Phoenician trader

Greek trireme

Sleek, fast, and deadly, the Greek trireme was one of the most powerful warships of the ancient world. The term "trireme" means "three oars," and this type of ship had three tiers of oars (upper, middle, and lower) on each side of the hull. Each oar was over 14 ft. (4 m) long. Together with a square sail, this gave the trireme an impressive turn of speed—either to get out of trouble or to make a hole in an enemy vessel with its fearsome ram.

Country: Mediterranean area
Date: c.1200 B.C.
Size: from 82 ft. (25 m) long
Construction: wood
Sail material: flax (linen)
On board: 30

Country: Greece
Date: c.480 B.C.
Size: 148 ft. (45 m) long
Construction: wood
Sail material: flax (linen)
On board: 190

Greek trireme

Roman galley

Roman warships were called galleys, and they could have two or three tiers of oars. The oarsmen were usually slaves or criminals. The Roman navy also used sails for extra speed, and they attacked their enemies by ramming. Galleys would also come alongside and throw out a wooden bridge for soldiers to swarm onto enemy ships.

Roman galley

Roman merchantman

Roman merchantman

The Romans needed large ships to carry goods around their huge empire. Their merchant ships were solidly built and broad. With one mast, usually rigged with a single, square sail, they were not very fast. However, they could carry up to 250 tons of cargo. There was extra space and height on the "poop deck" (aft—toward the rear).

Country: Mediterranean area
Date: 1st century B.C.
Size: 98 ft. (30 m) long
Construction: wood
Sail material: flax (linen)
On board: 30

Country: Mediterranean area
Date: 1st century B.C.
Size: 148 ft. (45 m) long
Construction: wood
Sail material: flax (linen)
On board: 120

Viking longship

These elegant ships with their decorated prows were feared for bringing Vikings on raids along the coasts of Europe. All had a single mast, a square sail, and up to 34 ports for oars on each side. Smaller versions were used along rivers and broader ones for cargo.

Viking longship

Country: Northern Europe area
Date: c.850 A.D.
Size: from 69 ft. (21 m) long
Construction: wood
Sail material: wool
On board: 34

Sailing to New Worlds

Sailing the uncharted oceans in the 1400s was like traveling to the planets today. Carracks, caravels, and similar sailing ships took European navigators to new worlds. Early sailing ships were small with square sails and lateen (triangular) sails, and sometimes both. The three-masted, square-rigged ship remained unchanged for several hundred years.

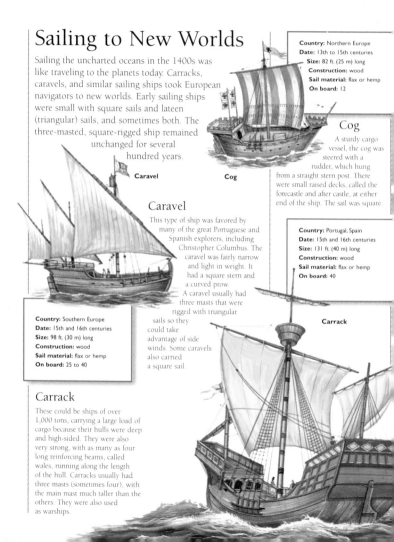

Caravel

Cog

Country: Northern Europe
Date: 13th to 15th centuries
Size: 82 ft. (25 m) long
Construction: wood
Sail material: flax or hemp
On board: 12

Cog

A sturdy cargo vessel, the cog was steered with a rudder, which hung from a straight stern post. There were small raised decks, called the forecastle and after castle, at either end of the ship. The sail was square.

Caravel

This type of ship was favored by many of the great Portuguese and Spanish explorers, including Christopher Columbus. The caravel was fairly narrow and light in weight. It had a square stern and a curved prow. A caravel usually had three masts that were rigged with triangular sails so they could take advantage of side winds. Some caravels also carried a square sail.

Country: Portugal, Spain
Date: 15th and 16th centuries
Size: 131 ft. (40 m) long
Construction: wood
Sail material: flax or hemp
On board: 40

Carrack

Country: Southern Europe
Date: 15th and 16th centuries
Size: 98 ft. (30 m) long
Construction: wood
Sail material: flax or hemp
On board: 25 to 40

Carrack

These could be ships of over 1,000 tons, carrying a large load of cargo because their hulls were deep and high-sided. They were also very strong, with as many as four long reinforcing beams, called wales, running along the length of the hull. Carracks usually had three masts (sometimes four), with the main mast much taller than the others. They were also used as warships.

Galleon

Galleons were tall fighting ships with elegant, pointed prows and high after castles that could be decorated with rich carving and gilding. They carried rows of cannons, which fired through square gun ports on the sides of the ship. The extra weight of these heavy guns could have made the galleon unstable, but the ship's inward-sloping sides helped keep it steady.

Country: Europe
Date: 17th century
Size: 125 ft. (38 m) long
Construction: wood
Sail material: flax or hemp
On board: 142

Galleon

Mayflower

The *Mayflower* was similar to a small galleon, but had only a handful of guns. The decks were used for cramming in supplies and passengers, early settlers of North America, known as the Pilgrims. The crew had a cabin and galley in the forecastle.

Mayflower

Country: Southern Europe
Date: 15th and 16th centuries
Size: 131 ft. (40 m) long
Construction: wood, clinker built
Sail material: flax or hemp
On board: 40 or more

Dutch East Indiaman

Country: Northern Europe
Date: 13th to 15th centuries
Size: 82 ft. (25 m) long
Construction: wood
Sail material: flax or hemp
On board: 12

Pinnace

Smaller than a galleon, a pinnace could either be rowed or sailed. It was a three-masted vessel with a large after castle and a tapering prow. The ship was square-rigged, but the rear mast could be rigged with just a triangular sail.

Pinnace

Country: Northern Europe
Date: 17th and 18th centuries
Size: 148 ft. (45 m) long
Construction: wood
Sail material: flax or hemp
On board: 45 or more

Dutch East Indiaman

The islands of Indonesia were known as the Spice Islands or the East Indies. Many European merchants traded there and in China and India. They used *East Indiamen* to bring back their cargoes. The ships had large hulls with plenty of cargo space. They had three masts and also carried many guns on their upper decks to protect themselves against attack.

Big Sailing Ships

From the 17th century, seafaring nations such as Britain and Holland began to acquire large worldwide empires. They needed larger ships to carry all sorts of cargoes—spices, tea, slaves, and sugar—to and from their colonies across the oceans. These bigger ships also carried more sails, making them faster and more maneuverable. Some of these vessels, such as the clippers, could sail from London to Shanghai in under 100 days.

Man-of-War

Country: Europe
Date: 18th to 19th centuries
Size: 394 ft. (120 m) long
Construction: wood
Sail fabric: flax or hemp
On board: 800

Endeavour

Endeavour

British Captain James Cook set off in 1768 for his explorations to the Pacific in a ship originally designed to carry coal in the rough North Sea. The solidly-built *Endeavour* had plenty of room in the hold for supplies, plant specimens, carvings, and other items Cook collected.

Country: Europe
Date: 18th century
Size: 131 ft. (40 m) long
Construction: wood
Sail fabric: flax or hemp
On board: 90

Man-of-War

These warships usually had between one and three decks of cannons. A three-decker could carry over 100 guns. They were designed to get the captain within range of the enemy so a "broadside" of cannonballs could be fired.

Frigate

Country: U.S.A.
Date: 19th century
Size: 180 ft. (55 m) long
Construction: wood
Sail fabric: cotton or hemp
On board: 28

Thomas W. Lawson

A schooner is a sailing ship with two or more masts and the lower sails rigged along the length of the vessel. Most were coastal or medium-range cargo vessels, but some were huge ocean-going schooners. The *Thomas W. Lawson* is the biggest ever built. She had seven masts, but used engines to help a very small crew hoist her sails.

Thomas W. Lawson

Frigate

Frigates carry their main weapons on a single deck. The US Navy designed large and speedy frigates to defend shipping from attacks by pirates—especially Barbary corsairs from North Africa. Some American frigates had 44 guns.

Country: U.S.A.
Date: 1902
Size: 395 ft. (120 m) long
Construction: wood planking on iron
Sail fabric: flax or hemp
On board: about 20

Barquentine

Square sails on the foremast and fore-and-aft rigging on the two rear masts identify barquentines. Rather long in proportion to their depth, they were graceful vessels. Because they had fewer square sails, they required smaller crews than full-rigged ships. They were popular in the Pacific when they were introduced in the 1830s, and were frequently seen on the Great Lakes of North America and canals that connected them.

Country: Europe, U.S.A.
Date: late 19th century
Size: 328 ft. (100 m) long
Construction: wood or steel
Sail fabric: flax, cotton, or hemp
On board: 30

Barquentine

Country: Europe, U.S.A.
Date: late 19th century
Size: 328 ft. (100 m) long
Construction: steel
Sail fabric: flax, cotton, or hemp
On board: 30

Four-masted barque

Four-masted barque

Ships like this continued to sail in the age of steam. They were large, square-sterned, and carried plenty of sail. Seamen gave the name "barque" to any vessel with non-square sails, rigged fore-and-aft (lengthwise) on the mizzen (rearmost) mast.

Clipper

Clipper

The clippers were the transportation record-breakers of their day. They were built to carry cargo at speed—supplies to the new communities of the California gold rush, and tea from China to Europe. Clippers had sleek bows, long narrow hulls, and up to about 30,000 sq. ft. (2,790 sq m) of sail. They could cover long distances in shorter times than any other sailing ship, for example, from Melbourne to London in under 80 days.

Country: U.S.A., Europe
Date: late 18th and 19th centuries
Size: 361 ft. (110 m) long
Construction: wood and iron
Sail fabric: flax, hemp, or cotton
On board: 45

Full Steam Ahead

For thousands of years, ships could only steer a course that the wind or oar power allowed. Then in the 19th century, the steam engine brought about a mechanical revolution in sea transportation. Steamships could steer almost any course at any time, and at a regular speed. The first steamship, *Pyroscaphe*, was built in France in 1783. Early steamships had paddle wheels. Propellers took over in the 1840s. Sails continued to be carried until the 1860s, when marine engines had become more reliable.

Charlotte Dundas

Country: Britain
Date: 1801
Size: 58 ft. (17.7 m) long
Construction: wood
Top speed: 4 mph (6.5 km/h)
On board: 6

Charlotte Dundas

The first practical steamship, the *Charlotte Dundas*, towed barges on the River Clyde in Scotland for three or four weeks in 1802. It was powered by a single-cylinder 12 horsepower engine driving a paddle wheel. The vessel was taken out-of-service because of damage to the river banks caused by the wash from its paddle wheel.

Great Western

The *Great Western* was built of oak and designed by Isambard Kingdom Brunel in 1837. It had four steam engines driving both paddle wheels and a propeller, and was the first ship to have enough coal for a nonstop voyage. It set out on its first transatlantic voyage on April 8, 1838, and docked in New York 15 days and 5 hours later.

Country: Britain
Date: 1837
Size: 236 ft. (72 m) long
Construction: wood, iron reinforcements
Top speed: 10 mph (15.75 km/h)
On board: 148

Great Western

Savannah

The *Savannah* was the first steamship to cross the Atlantic Ocean. It was a sailing vessel equipped with steam engines and paddle wheels. It made its historic voyage from Savannah, Georgia, to Liverpool in 27 days. Its wood-burning engines were used to drive two paddle wheels for only a small part of the crossing, but enough to prove that steamships were practical ocean-going vessels.

Savannah

Country: U.S.A.
Date: 1819
Size: 98 ft. (30 m) long
Construction: wood
Top speed: 9 mph (15 km/h)
On board: 42

Country: Britain
Date: 1858
Size: 692 ft. (211 m) long
Construction: wood
Top speed: 15 mph (24 km/h)
On board: 4,000

Britannia

Britannia

Britannia was a wooden paddle steamer and the first transatlantic passenger liner. Its ocean service began in 1840. As part of a fleet of passenger steamers, it offered a twice-monthly passage all year round between Liverpool and Boston.

Country: Britain
Date: 1840
Size: 212 ft. (64.7 m) long
Construction: wood
Top speed: 10 mph (15.75 km/h)
On board: 204

Country: Britain
Date: 1856
Size: 377 ft. (115 m) long
Construction: iron
Top speed: 15½ mph (25 km/h)
On board: 250

Persia

Great Britain

Brunel's second transatlantic ship was also the first iron-hulled steamship. He designed it with paddle wheels, but they were changed to a propeller. In 1970, its rusting hull was brought to the docks where it was originally built, and restored.

Persia

The *Persia* was the world's largest liner until the *Great Eastern* was built. It was also one of the last to be powered by paddles—they were huge at 40 ft. (12 m) across—rather than by a screw propeller.

Great Eastern

When the *Great Eastern* was built, it was five times the size of any other ship. It was powered by a screw propeller and paddle wheels, and carried enough coal to reach Australia without refueling. It failed as a liner, but successfully laid the first transatlantic telegraph cable in 1866 on its second attempt.

Country: Britain
Date: 1843
Size: 322 ft. (98 m) long
Construction: iron
Top speed: 13 mph (20 km/h)
On board: 260

Great Britain

Great Eastern

Luxury Liners

Steamships began carrying passengers and mail across the Atlantic in 1838. By the 1890s, liners were designed to accommodate hundreds of passengers in the sort of luxury usually found in the best hotels. Swimming pools, dance-floors, opulent lounges, and restaurants catered to the wealthy first-class travelers. Below water, a row of watertight bulkheads (walls) stretched across each vessel, dividing it into separate compartments to keep it afloat if one part of the hull was damaged. Modern cruise ships carry 4.5 million people every year.

Turbinia

This was the first vessel to be driven by a steam turbine. In this type of engine, high-pressure steam pushes on a series of blades that are set on a metal shaft. When the blades move, the shaft turns, making the ship's propeller spin around.

Turbinia

Country: Britain
Date: 1894
Size: 105 ft. (32 m) long
Construction: steel
Top speed: 32¼ mph (61 km/h)
On board: 5

King Edward

The first merchant ship to be powered by the kind of turbines used in the *Turbinia* was the *King Edward*. The vessel's powerful engines propelled the ship on passenger services up and down the River Clyde and on cruises along the Scottish coast. The ship was used to carry troops during World War II.

Country: Britain
Date: 1901
Size: 328 ft. (100 m) long
Construction: steel
Top speed: 23½ mph (38 km/h)
On board: 200

King Edward

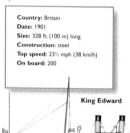

Titanic

With interiors based on a French royal palace, the *Titanic* was very luxurious. It was the largest ship of the time. But on April 15, 1912, on its maiden voyage, it hit an iceberg and sank in the Atlantic Ocean off the coast of Newfoundland. There were too few lifeboats and 1,500 people drowned. Now all ships have to carry enough lifeboats and life jackets for all those on board.

Titanic

Bremen

The German-built *Bremen* was designed to be the fastest transatlantic liner. The record had been set 20 years before by Britain's *Mauretania* at 26 mph (48 km/h). *Bremen* beat the record. It was also more spacious than its rival, with an extra 131 ft. (40 m) of hull space for the same number of passengers and crew.

Country: Germany
Date: 1929
Size: 938 ft. (286 m) long
Construction: steel
Top speed: 28 mph (52 km/h)
On board: 2,990

Bremen

Country: Britain
Date: 1912
Size: 853 ft. (260 m) long
Construction: steel
Top speed: 22 mph (41 km/h)
On board: 3,511

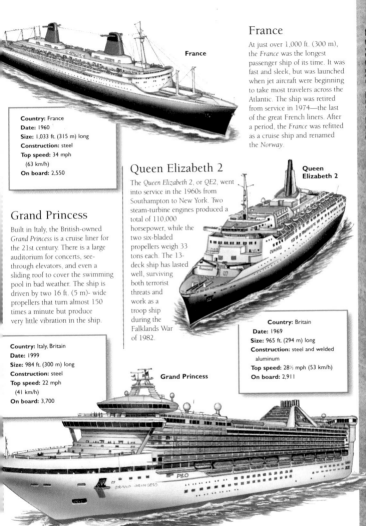

France

At just over 1,000 ft. (300 m), the *France* was the longest passenger ship of its time. It was fast and sleek, but was launched when jet aircraft were beginning to take most travelers across the Atlantic. The ship was retired from service in 1974—the last of the great French liners. After a period, the *France* was refitted as a cruise ship and renamed the *Norway*.

France

Country: France
Date: 1960
Size: 1,033 ft. (315 m) long
Construction: steel
Top speed: 34 mph
(63 km/h)
On board: 2,550

Queen Elizabeth 2

The *Queen Elizabeth 2*, or QE2, went into service in the 1960s from Southampton to New York. Two steam-turbine engines produced a total of 110,000 horsepower, while the two six-bladed propellers weigh 33 tons each. The 13-deck ship has lasted well, surviving both terrorist threats and work as a troop ship during the Falklands War of 1982.

Queen Elizabeth 2

Country: Britain
Date: 1969
Size: 965 ft. (294 m) long
Construction: steel and welded aluminum
Top speed: 28½ mph (53 km/h)
On board: 2,911

Grand Princess

Built in Italy, the British-owned *Grand Princess* is a cruise liner for the 21st century. There is a large auditorium for concerts, see-through elevators, and even a sliding roof to cover the swimming pool in bad weather. The ship is driven by two 16 ft. (5 m)- wide propellers that turn almost 150 times a minute but produce very little vibration in the ship.

Country: Italy, Britain
Date: 1999
Size: 984 ft. (300 m) long
Construction: steel
Top speed: 22 mph
(41 km/h)
On board: 3,700

Grand Princess

Warships

With the coming of steam power, the way the warships looked and operated changed. Sails and wooden hulls were replaced with screw propellers and iron hulls. Warships became faster, easier to maneuver, and had more space for newer and bigger guns that fired explosive shells. Modern navies use a variety of different craft, from huge aircraft carriers to smaller multitask ships.

Warrior

Driven by both steam and sail, the *Warrior* was the first ocean-going, iron-clad battleship in the world. Thick-armored plates were bolted to a teak hull to give massive protection. The ship also carried 36 powerful guns, making it the most heavily armed ship at the time.

Merrimack

Monitor

Warrior

Merrimack v. Monitor

The Civil War (1861–65) saw the first battle between metal-armored, steam-driven ships. The North's all-iron battleship *Monitor* lay low in the water, bearing a single turret with two guns. The South's *Merrimack* was fitted with sloping iron armor over its deck. The four-hour battle ended in a stalemate.

Country: U.S.A.
Date: 1862
Size: *Monitor* 172 ft. (52 m) long;
Merrimack 263 ft. (80 m) long
Construction: wood, iron armour
Top speed: *Monitor* 6 mph (11 km/h);
Merrimack 9 mph (17 km/h)
On board: *Monitor* 49;
Merrimack 330

Country: Britain
Date: 1859
Size: 420 ft. (116 m) long
Construction: wood, iron armour
Top speed: 17 mph (31.5 km/h)
On board: 707

Dreadnought

The steel-plated *Dreadnought* was the first modern battleship. It had heavy guns mounted on five turrets that could be fired at the same time. A telephone linked each turret to a control platform.

Lightning

Torpedo missiles that travel underwater to their target were developed in the 1860s and 1870s. Navies quickly set about building ships to fire torpedoes. The *Lightning* was one of the first British torpedo boats and was also used to defend coastal bases from enemy attack.

Lightning

Country: Britain
Date: 1877
Size: 84 ft. (26 m) long
Construction: wood
Top speed: 20 mph (33 km/h)
On board: 35

Country: Britain
Date: 1906
Size: 526 ft. (160 m) long
Construction: steel
Top speed: 21 mph (39 km/h)
On board: 773

Dreadnought

Yamato

In the late 1930s this vast Japanese World War II battleship was the largest-ever warship—only the liner *Queen Mary* was heavier. The ship could therefore have many guns. On the main turrets alone, there were nine guns, each of which could fire two heavy shells per minute up to a distance of 25 mi. (40 km).

Yamato

Country: Japan
Date: 1937
Size: 862 ft. (263 m) long
Construction: steel
Top speed: 27 mph (50 km/h)
On board: 2,500

MEKO-class frigate

Escort vessels, such as the MEKO series, are used to protect aircraft carriers, groups of submarines, or convoys of ships. The name is an abbreviation for a German word meaning "multi-purpose." The basic hull is designed so the different weapons and equipment can be put in when needed.

MEKO-class frigate

Country: Germany
Date: 1980s
Size: 299 ft. (91.2 m) long
Construction: steel
Top speed: 27 mph (50 km/h)
On board: 90

USS Virginia

The warship USS *Virginia* was powered by a nuclear reactor. The reactor heats water to produce steam, which drives a turbine as in a regular steamship. The advantage of nuclear power is that the vessel can sail vast distances without having to stop for fuel: one fueling alone can take such a ship three times around the world. However, there is a big safety risk, in spite of the fact that on-board reactors have protective shields weighing as much as 1,000 tons. In addition, only a few specialized depots can make repairs to this type of ship.

USS Virginia

Country: U.S.A.
Date: 1974
Size: 585 ft. (178.3 m) long
Construction: steel
Top speed: 30 mph (56 km/h)
On board: 578

Powerboats

Powered craft can be anything from a small dinghy with an outboard motor to a high-speed racing vessel. But for most people a "powerboat" means a racing craft built for speeds of up to 57 mph (90 km/h) or more. There are many types, but most are made with planing hulls—in other words, they are designed to rise up out of the water as they pick up speed, to reduce drag and help them go even faster. They are often built with modern materials, such as layers of fiberglass sandwiched with lightweight balsa wood. This cuts down on weight and improves performance even more.

Water-jet engine

A water-jet engine takes in water through a duct and forces it out at speed, and at high pressure, through the stern of the unit. The result is that the boat is pushed forward in the opposite direction to the jet of water.

Around-the-world power record

The slender hull of the *Cable & Wireless Adventurer* is designed to slice through the waves at up to 28 mph (45 km/h). Its twin turbodiesel engines are powerful and efficient, cutting down the need for refueling. With 16 crew members, the 115-ft. (35-m), 52-ton powerboat set off in April 1998 to break the around-the-world record for a motor-powered vessel. It took 75 days, and the craft cut 9 days off the previous record.

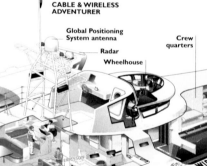

CABLE & WIRELESS ADVENTURER

Aerial

Global Positioning System antenna

Radar

Wheelhouse

Crew quarters

Rubber dinghy

Galley

8.3 liter turbo-diesel engine

Rudders

Propeller

62

VSVs

The *VSV* (Very Slender Vessel) is a powerboat with a long, thin hull with deep and narrow sides. These give both stability and sharp turning in the water. The *VSV* tends to push or pierce its way in and under the waves rather than riding over them, which makes its passage both fast and smooth. The vessel is designed to be used by coastal police patrols and special military forces.

Hull shapes

Powerboat hulls are designed to offer little resistance as they move through the water, so they can reach the highest possible speeds. One way to achieve this is to make a very slim single hull, or monohull, that slices through the waves. Creating a twin-hulled boat, or catamaran, also cuts down on the amount of contact between hulls and water, reducing friction. Hydroplanes solve the problem by rising right up out of the water, skimming over the surface with the least drag, or resistance.

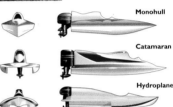

Monohull

Catamaran

Hydroplane

Powerboat types

Powerboats can be pleasure craft designed to carry one or more people and to give them a taste of speed. Offshore racers go faster, and even monohull designs lift out of the water as they reach top speed. Hydroplanes race at speeds of over 100 mph (160 km/h), while powerful Formula One craft have 300 horsepower engines capable of 125 mph (200 km/h) and sharp right-angled turns.

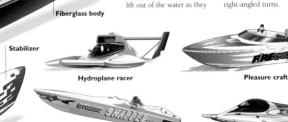

Wave-piercing hull

CABLE & WIRELESS

Fiberglass body

Stabilizer

Hydroplane racer

Pleasure craft

Offshore racer

Formula One racer

Underwater Vessels

Any submarine craft needs a strong hull to withstand the pressure deep underwater, and a tube-shaped design to cut through it with least resistance. The largest underwater craft are nuclear submarines with powerful engines that can travel far away from base without refueling. Smaller underwater vessels, known as submersibles, are used for scientific and shipwreck exploration, as well as for checking oil rigs and making repairs below the water.

Nautilus

Country: U.S.A.
Date: 1800
Size: 21 ft. (6.4 m) long
Construction: iron framework, copper outer covering
Top speed: 4 mph (6.5 km/h) underwater
On board: 3

Nautilus

This strange craft was powered by sail on the surface and by a hand-cranked propeller underwater. It was invented by American Robert Fulton, and tested in France, where it stayed underwater for an hour. The aim was to use *Nautilus* to attach explosives to the hulls of enemy ships, but the craft was never used in naval warfare.

Holland No. 6

Country: U.S.A.
Date: 1897
Size: 153 ft. (16.3 m) long
Construction: iron
Top speed: 9 mph (15 km/h) underwater
On board: 7

Holland No. 6

Irish-American engineer James Holland's *No. 6* was called a "monster war fish" in the American press. It was the first modern submarine, and boasted ballast tanks, torpedo tubes, and a periscope that could be retracted when the craft dived (features that were used on nearly all the later submarines). It had hydroplanes (fins) to help move up and down.

Country: France
Date: 1893
Size: 159 ft. (48.5 m) long
Construction: copper
Top speed: 7½ mph (12 km/h) underwater
On board: 19

Gustave Zédé

This was the first submarine to be equipped with a periscope, which allowed the captain and the crew to view the surface of the water while they were still submerged. One of the first effective submarines, this sleek vessel was driven by an electric motor powered by huge batteries.

Gustave Zédé

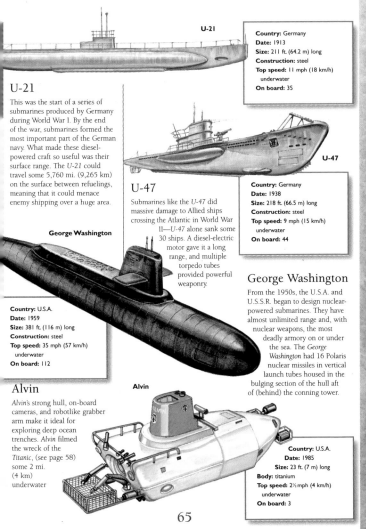

U-21

Country: Germany
Date: 1913
Size: 211 ft. (64.2 m) long
Construction: steel
Top speed: 11 mph (18 km/h) underwater
On board: 35

U-21

This was the start of a series of submarines produced by Germany during World War I. By the end of the war, submarines formed the most important part of the German navy. What made these diesel-powered craft so useful was their surface range. The *U-21* could travel some 5,760 mi. (9,265 km) on the surface between refuelings, meaning that it could menace enemy shipping over a huge area.

U-47

U-47

Submarines like the *U-47* did massive damage to Allied ships crossing the Atlantic in World War II—*U-47* alone sank some 30 ships. A diesel-electric motor gave it a long range, and multiple torpedo tubes provided powerful weaponry.

Country: Germany
Date: 1938
Size: 218 ft. (66.5 m) long
Construction: steel
Top speed: 9 mph (15 km/h) underwater
On board: 44

George Washington

George Washington

From the 1950s, the U.S.A. and U.S.S.R. began to design nuclear-powered submarines. They have almost unlimited range and, with nuclear weapons, the most deadly armory on or under the sea. The *George Washington* had 16 Polaris nuclear missiles in vertical launch tubes housed in the bulging section of the hull aft of (behind) the conning tower.

Country: U.S.A.
Date: 1959
Size: 381 ft. (116 m) long
Construction: steel
Top speed: 35 mph (57 km/h) underwater
On board: 112

Alvin

Alvin's strong hull, on-board cameras, and robotlike grabber arm make it ideal for exploring deep ocean trenches. *Alvin* filmed the wreck of the *Titanic*, (see page 58) some 2 mi. (4 km) underwater

Alvin

Country: U.S.A.
Date: 1985
Size: 23 ft. (7 m) long
Body: titanium
Top speed: 2½ mph (4 km/h) underwater
On board: 3

Cargo Carriers

Ships that carry cargo are called merchant ships, and there are a huge variety of these vessels on the seas today. They range from vast oil tankers to tiny tugs, from car-carrying ferries to ships specially built to recover other damaged ships. They may be slow, but they can carry much larger amounts of goods and raw materials than any other form of transportation—and at very low costs—anywhere in the world. Cargo ships have very little superstructure (the part above the main deck level). There is a navigation bridge with funnels, and the engines and crew accommodations are below. The rest of the ship holds as much cargo as possible.

Gas tanker

When gases are refrigerated under pressure, they turn to liquid. Large gas tankers, carrying liquid gas in big, spherical tanks, became common during the 1970s. Such tankers can contain up to 4.5 million cu. ft. of liquid gas. These ships ply the oceans, notably between Australia and Japan.

Gas tanker

Country: Netherlands
Date: 1973
Size: 318 ft. (97 m) long
Construction: steel
Top speed: 12 mph (22 km/h)
On board: 20

Supertanker

The world's largest ships can weigh half a million tons and are so huge that they need several miles to slow down and stop. They carry oil in several vast tanks, which have to be separated to prevent the oil from surging in heavy seas and possibly capsizing.

Supertanker

Country: Norway
Date: 1978
Size: 1,475 ft. (450 m) long
Construction: steel
Top speed: 14 mph (26 km/h)
On board: 18

Container ship

Instead of carrying all sorts of goods of many awkward shapes, container vessels carry 20 ft. or 40 ft. (6 m or 12 m) long metal containers, which fit exactly onto both ships and trucks. The strong containers are stacked in piles of up to 13, and each container can take more than 21 tons of cargo.

Container ship

Country: Spain
Date: 1974
Size: 300 ft. (91 m) long
Construction: steel
Top speed: 14 mph (26 km/h)
On board: 20

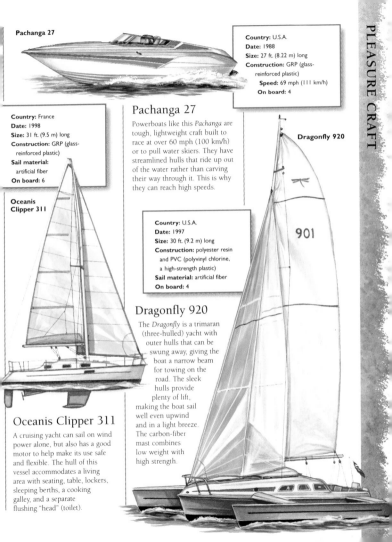

Pachanga 27

Country: U.S.A.
Date: 1988
Size: 27 ft. (8.22 m) long
Construction: GRP (glass-reinforced plastic)
Speed: 69 mph (111 km/h)
On board: 4

Pachanga 27

Powerboats like this *Pachanga* are tough, lightweight craft built to race at over 60 mph (100 km/h) or to pull water skiers. They have streamlined hulls that ride up out of the water rather than carving their way through it. This is why they can reach high speeds.

Dragonfly 920

Country: France
Date: 1998
Size: 31 ft. (9.5 m) long
Construction: GRP (glass-reinforced plastic)
Sail material: artificial fiber
On board: 6

Oceanis Clipper 311

Country: U.S.A.
Date: 1997
Size: 30 ft. (9.2 m) long
Construction: polyester resin and PVC (polyvinyl chloride, a high-strength plastic)
Sail material: artificial fiber
On board: 4

Dragonfly 920

The *Dragonfly* is a trimaran (three-hulled) yacht with outer hulls that can be swung away, giving the boat a narrow beam for towing on the road. The sleek hulls provide plenty of lift, making the boat sail well even upwind and in a light breeze. The carbon-fiber mast combines low weight with high strength.

Oceanis Clipper 311

A cruising yacht can sail on wind power alone, but also has a good motor to help make its use safe and flexible. The hull of this vessel accommodates a living area with seating, table, lockers, sleeping berths, a cooking galley, and a separate flushing "head" (toilet).

New Horizons

Ever since the first boats took to the water, the challenge for the adventurous sailor has been to travel faster and farther. The great age of racing began in the 19th century when wealthy enthusiasts started to build yachts especially for this purpose. Racing yachts today use space-age materials for everything from keels to sails and rely on satellite navigation to find their way. Technological improvements mean people can attempt new feats such as solo around-the-world races, breaking speed records, or using muscle power to cross oceans.

Francis Chichester began yacht racing in 1953. By 1960 he had won the first-ever solo yacht race across the Atlantic Ocean in his boat **Gipsy Moth III**. He followed up this triumph in 1966–67 with the first solo voyage around the world in **Gipsy Moth IV**, taking a total of 226 days.

Donald Campbell was one of the world's great speed-record breakers. In 1964, driving his hydroplane **Bluebird**, he reached 276¼ mph (444.7 km/h) on Lake Dumbleyung, Australia. He was killed in 1967 when his boat crashed at 320 mph (515 km/h).

Jason Lewis is the first person to attempt to pedal around the world. Part of his trip was overland, but he also completed the first crossing of the Pacific in a pedal-powered boat in August 2000. **Moksha** is only 26 ft. (8 m) long, with a cabin the size of a small closet. Solar panels power a computer, a satellite telephone, and a Global Positioning System.

The most sought-after prize in yacht racing, the America's Cup, is named after the yacht that first won it in 1851. This elegant J-class schooner, **Endeavour**, just failed to win the cup in 1934.

The SeaCat **Hoverspeed Great Britain** traveled across the Atlantic Ocean in 3 days, 7 hours, and 54 minutes in 1990—the fastest-ever crossing.

The first boat in the grueling Whitbread Round-the-World Race to have an all-woman crew was **Maiden**, a 57 ft. (17.5 m) sloop. Many said the 31,980 mi. (51,500 km) race was too hard for women, but skipper **Tracy Edwards** and her crew proved them wrong. They not only finished the 1989 race, but won two of the stages in their class.

On the Tracks

Railroads are the most efficient way to move large numbers of people and heavy cargoes, and cause the least damage to the environment.

The first railroads were simple grooved tracks, carved in stone blocks and used in Babylon in about 2245 B.C. Later, horses dragged coal wagons along simple wooden rails until the invention of the steam locomotive 200 years ago. Today, a modern freight train hauled by a diesel or electric locomotive can do the same job as over 50 trucks, and a high-speed passenger train can carry the same number of people as 200 cars, in greater comfort and at higher speeds.

Powerful steel wheels with connecting and coupling rods help drive this **Chinese steam locomotive**. China has more railroad lines than anywhere in the world, and it is still building steam locomotives—50 years after most other countries turned to diesel and electric power because they are much cleaner and more efficient.

Burlington Zephyr 1934

What is a train?

Rails

Ballast

Rail tracks are bolted or clipped onto wooden, concrete, or steel **ties**. These are laid into a **track bed** of hard stones, which is called a ballast.

A train is made up of the locomotive (engine), which pulls the rolling stock (passenger cars or freight). Trains are powered by electricity, diesel, or steam engines, and mainly run on steel rails bolted to the ground. Railroads are still the most efficient way to carry large numbers of passengers or huge amounts of goods overland.

Locomotives ride on two rails, but some electric trains draw their power from a **third rail**, laid between or alongside the normal tracks.

Steam locomotive

By the 20th century, steam locomotives were quite complex machines. Coal from the tender at the rear would be shoveled into the firebox, where it was burned to heat the water in the boiler. This is turned into steam, which was forced at high pressure into the cylinders at the front of the engine. Pistons inside the cylinders are connected to long rods which turn the large driving wheels. The trolley of wheels is called a bogie (see page 87). The buffers at each end of the locomotive and at the end of the rail track help reduce the shock caused upon contact.

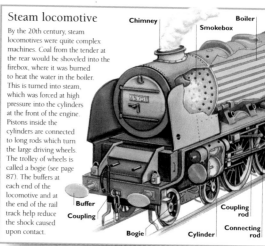

Chimney **Boiler** **Smokebox** **Buffer** **Coupling** **Coupling rod** **Bogie** **Cylinder** **Connecting rod**

Power source

Diesel power and electricity took over from steam in the 1950s, offering more power and easier maintenance. A diesel locomotive has an engine positioned between two driving cabs, while the electric draws power from overhead wires or a third rail, and equipment inside converts this into energy that powers the wheels.

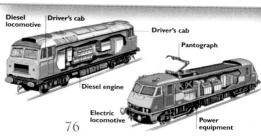

Diesel locomotive **Driver's cab** **Driver's cab** **Pantograph** **Diesel engine** **Electric locomotive** **Power equipment**

Driver's cab

While a train is not steered like a car because it travels on fixed rails, the driver still has to operate several levers to keep it moving. The dials on the dashboard indicate speed, the working of the brakes, how much power is being supplied from the diesel engine or electricity source, and alert the driver to faults with car lights and automatic doors.

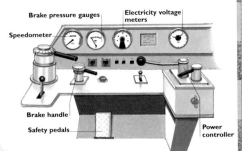

Brake pressure gauges
Electricity voltage meters
Speedometer
Brake handle
Safety pedals
Power controller

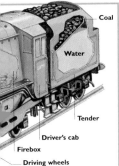

Coal
Water
Tender
Driver's cab
Firebox
Driving wheels

Today, only China, India, and South Africa remain as regular users of steam locomotives. They are very expensive to run and need to be taken out of service regularly to clean out the ash and soot.

Types of engine

In addition to passenger and freight trains, there are many other types of engines running on the tracks. At night and on weekends, workmen repair or relay track and check that signals are working properly. Special engineering trains include cranes built on wagons, huge mechanical diggers that clean the ballast (the stones under the track), and ensure the rails are the correct distance apart. Breakdown trains are kept at major depots ready to turn out in an emergency. In winter, snowplows and snowblowers are placed at the front of locomotives to clear the path for trains to run normally.

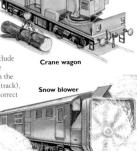

Crane wagon

Snow blower

Ballast cleaning train

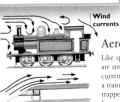

Wind currents

Aerodynamics

Like sports cars, trains go faster if they are streamlined. In strong headwinds, the currents sweep effortlessly over the top of a train with a sloping front instead of being trapped, as happens with locomotives with flat front ends. This does not matter much, however, with slow-moving local trains or freights.

77

Running on Rails

When rails were first laid in stone quarries and coal mines, horses hauled the wagons. However, the wars against Napoleon of France (1799–1815) left Britain with a shortage of these animals. It was the search for a "mechanical horse" that led to the invention of the steam locomotive. From the late 1820s, locomotives were running on tracks in Britain and the U.S. By 1840, almost 1,500 mi. (2,400 km) of track had been completed in Britain, and in 1869 a golden spike was driven into the final track of the completed American transcontinental railroad.

Rocket

Country: Britain
Date: 1829
Size: 20 ft. (6 m) long
Construction: iron and wood
Top speed: 29 mph (47 km/h)
Number built: 1

Trevithick

The world's first steam locomotive to run on rails was built by British engineer Richard Trevithick for the Coalbrookdale Ironworks in Shropshire. It had flat, tired wheels, and was so heavy that it broke the cast-iron rails. But his basic idea of directing the engine's exhaust steam up a chimney became the standard design.

Trevithick

Country: Britain
Date: 1803
Size: 15 ft. (4.5 m) long
Construction: iron and wood
Top speed: 3 mph (5 km/h)
Number built: 1

Rocket

The Liverpool & Manchester Railway held a competition in 1829 for the best locomotive before it opened in 1830. Robert and George Stephenson's *Rocket* was the winner. It hauled some of the world's very first passenger trains. The design of the *Rocket* also introduced new boiler, exhaust, firebox, and simpler drive features that were used in many later steam locomotives.

Locomotion No. 1

George Stephenson designed *Locomotion* for the Stockton & Darlington Railway in 1825. It was the first engine to have its driving wheels joined together with connecting rods to make sure they turned at the same speed and gave extra grip on slopes.

Country: Britain
Date: 1825
Size: 20 ft. (6 m) long
Construction: iron and wood
Top speed: 15 mph (24 km/h)
Number built: 1

Locomotion No. 1

Lion

Lion

Still going strong after 160 years, *Lion* is Britain's oldest working locomotive. This six-wheeler was built for the Liverpool & Manchester Railway, and it was rediscovered in the 1920s being used as a pumping engine. It was carefully restored to its original condition. *Lion* is taken out for special events and is kept at the Manchester Museum of Science & Technology.

Country: Britain
Date: 1838
Size: 26 ft. (8 m) long
Construction: iron and wood
Top speed: 45 mph (70 km/h)
Number built: 2

Stirling No. 1

Patrick Stirling, engineer of Britain's Great Northern Railway from 1866 to 1895, was as concerned about how his locomotives looked as he was about how they performed. His *No. 1* was an express engine for the East Coast Main Line, and its single set of driving wheels were an amazing 8 ft. (2.5 m) high. *No. 1* became outclassed as trains got longer and heavier, but survives today as one of the most prized exhibits at the National Railway Museum in York.

Stirling No. 1

Country: Britain
Date: 1870
Size: 51 ft. (16 m) long
Construction: steel
Top speed: 75 mph (120 km/h)
Number built: 53

Woodburner

Until the 1870s, wood, not coal, was the fuel of steam locomotives in the U.S., because it was plentiful and cheap. The wide smokestack could catch the hot embers that might cause trackside fires. The "cowcatcher" was a frame at the front to push cattle off the track.

Woodburner

Country: U.S.A., Canada
Date: 1880
Size: 40 ft. (12 m) long
Construction: steel and iron
Top speed: 45 mph (70 km/h)
Number built: over 1,000

Steam-driven Trains

Steam locomotives were the dominant form of mass passenger and freight transportation throughout the 19th century and the first half of the 20th century. The trains got streamlined and faster—the American *No. 999* was the first to reach 100 mph (160 km/h). They also grew heavier—"Big Boys" had the strength of 7,000 horses and weighed 500 tons. But from the 1950s, steam was on the decline.

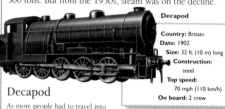

Decapod

Country: Britain
Date: 1902
Size: 32 ft. (10 m) long
Construction: steel
Top speed: 70 mph (110 km/h)
On board: 2 crew

Country: Britain
Date: 1896
Size: 25 ft. (8 m) long
Construction: steel
Top speed: 20 mph (30 km/h)
On board: 2 crew

Snowdon Mountain Railway

Rack engines (running on tooth-shape tracks to prevent slipping) began on Mt. Washington in 1869. They are a common sight today in the Alps, and in Wales, where this train made the first steep climb to the summit of Mt. Snowdon in 1896.

Decapod

As more people had to travel into cities to work, longer and faster trains were needed. The Great Eastern Railway experimented with the *Decapod*, a monster 10-wheeler that could accelerate rapidly away from the station. But only one was built because it was far too heavy to go over bridges safely.

Pannier

Country: Britain
Date: from 1929
Size: 32 ft. (10 m) long
Construction: steel
Top speed: 60 mph (37 km/h)
On board: 2 crew

Country: southern Africa
Date: 1955
Size: 100 ft. (31 m) long
Construction: steel
Top speed: 60 mph (100 km/h)
On board: 2 crew

Garratt

The *Garratt* was an odd-looking engine that had the boiler in the middle of the engine, with the tank at the front and the coal tender behind. It works like a modern semitractor rig—the main frame has a hinge in the middle to allow it to go around tight curves. Over 2,000 were built in Manchester for export all over the world, and many are still in use in southern Africa today.

Pannier

Named after the large water tanks slung over the top of the boiler like a pannier the *Pannier* replaced a mixed collection of elderly Victorian locomotives. A total of 1,200 were built as local passenger trains and short-distance freights. They were also used as shunting wagons in station yards in the West of England until replaced by diesels.

Garratt

"Q1" 0-6-0

One of Britain's ugliest steam engines, the sturdy "Q1" 0-6-0 was built during World War II (1939–45) when there was no money to spend on its appearance. All the working parts were easy to reach, and the "Q1" could haul heavy freight over any route. The first "Q1" is still working in the south of England on a heritage railway.

"Q1" 0-6-0

Country: Britain
Date: 1942
Size: 55 ft. (17 m) long
Construction: steel
Top speed: 70 mph (45 km/h)
On board: 2 crew

Mallard

The all-time world speed record for steam power was achieved by the streamlined *Mallard* on July 3, 1938. The sloping front end was inspired by the *Bugatti* racing car and the train reached a top racing speed of 126 mph (202 km/h). The engine is now in the National Railway Museum in York, England.

Mallard

Country: Britain
Date: 1938
Size: 71 ft. (22 m) long
Construction: steel
Top speed: 126 mph (201 km/h)
On board: 2 crew

"Big Boy"

The world's largest steam engines were the massive "Big Boys." They were built for the Union Pacific Railroad to haul 4,000-ton freight trains through the Wasatch Mountains in Utah. They stood 16 ft. (5 m) high, and had 24 wheels (16 to drive the train).

Country: U.S.A.
Date: from 1941 to 1956
Size: 131¼ ft. (40 m) long
Construction: steel
Top speed: 80 mph (129 km/h)
On board: 2 crew

"Big Boy"

Diesel-powered Trains

Because all their working parts are enclosed inside a large steel box, diesel locomotives tend to look the same all over the world and are not as glamorous as steam trains. But they are cleaner, require less servicing or refueling and can be easily added to, in order to pull the heaviest transcontinental trains. Diesel engines power generators in the locomotive, which provide electricity for the special motors that turn the wheels.

10000

Country: Britain
Date: 1948
Size: 61 ft. (19 m) long
Construction: steel
Top speed: 93 mph (150 km/h)
On board: 2 crew

10000

Britain's first main-line diesel was built as an experiment to compare its performance against the biggest express steam locomotives. The diesel won easily. Looking like American engines, *10000* and its sister *10001* were coupled together and covered almost 1 million mi. (1.6 million km).

Burlington Zephyr

Burlington Zephyr

This silver-colored sleek machine was the world's first diesel-electric streamlined train. It was designed to carry the very rich, and made its Denver-to-Chicago run of 1,000 mi. (1,600 km) nonstop in 13 hours. There was only room for 50 passengers in the three vehicles that made up the train because of the equipment inside.

Country: U.S.A.
Date: 1934
Size: 196 ft. (60 m) long
Construction: steel
Top speed: 104 mph (167 km/h)
On board: 2 crew

Country: U.S.A.
Date: 1941
Size: 33 ft. (10 m) long
Construction: steel
Top speed: 46 mph (74 km/h)
On board: 2 crew

Deltic

The *Deltics* packed 3,300 horsepower into their small bodies making them the world's most powerful diesel-electric locomotive in the 1950s. They were chosen by British Railways to speed up the London-Edinburgh expresses. The original locomotive was painted to look like an American engine.

Whitcomb

Whitcomb

Many European countries were desperate for new trains to replace those destroyed during fighting in World War II. American train builder Whitcomb came to the rescue with 200 trains, so well built that many of them are still working 60 years later. In Italy, they shunt carriages, while in France they are used in factory sidings. Despite their fairly small size, they are both powerful and easy to drive.

Country: Britain
Date: 1955
Size: 66 ft. (20 m) long
Construction: steel
Top speed: 100 mph (160 km/h)
On board: 2 crew

Deltic

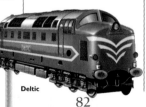

82

V200

V200

German designers devised this "diesel hydraulic" locomotive that had an automatic transmission and a complicated series of drive shafts to transfer the power from the engine to turn the wheels. Despite looking stylish and being reliable, it was very complicated and expensive to run, and was only in service for 20 years. Similar engines ran in Britain, too.

Country: Germany
Date: 1953
Size: 50 ft. (15 m) long
Construction: steel, aluminum
Top speed: 75 mph (120 km/h)
On board: 2 crew

M62

Russia built over 5,000 of the M62 diesels for use at home and abroad. However, many of those sent to East European countries have been scrapped because they are worn out and unreliable. Their engines smoked so badly that station staff said they needed to wear gas masks when an M62 arrived. Also, M62s cannot haul passenger cars in winter because they have no heating equipment.

Country: Russia, Hungary
Date: 1965
Size: 57 ft. (18 m) long
Construction: steel
Top speed: 60 mph (100 km/h)
On board: 2 crew

M62

SD40-2

Although it is rather noisy, the SD40-2 is regarded as the most reliable heavy-duty diesel locomotive ever built, and many hundreds can be seen around the world. Colors and markings vary, depending on which company owns it. In the U.S., their home country, three or four of them are often coupled together to haul freight trains that can be several miles long.

Country: U.S.A.
Date: 1980
Size: 69 ft. (21 m) long
Construction: steel
Top speed: 65 mph (105 km/h)
On board: 2 crew

SD40-2

Electric Trains

Electric trains are powered from a pantograph
(a sprung arm on the roof). It picks up the electricity
from overhead lines strung up between steel masts
along the track, or from a special third rail placed
next to the normal track. An electric motor either inside
the locomotive or underneath the car turns the driving
wheels. Trains driven by electricity are more powerful than
diesel and steam, and accelerate much faster.
Electricity is also a cleaner fuel.

Early electric

Country: Britain
Date: from 1904
Size: 53 ft. (16 m) long
Construction: steel
Top speed: 90 mph (145 km/h)
On board: 2 crew

Early electric

Britain's first electric locomotives
were built by the North Eastern
Railway (NER) to haul coal around
the Newcastle area. They only ran
for 20 years because they were too
complicated and expensive to run.
Coal was still very cheap to buy, so
the NER went back to steam trains.

Crocodile

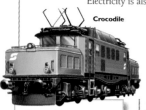

Crocodile

Some of the earliest electric
locomotives built for Germany
and Austria were nicknamed
"Crocodiles" because of their
narrow front ends, two cab
windows that looked like large
eyes, and connected driving
wheels that looked like
gnashing teeth. They were
extremely powerful engines,
and hauled the heaviest
passenger and freight
trains for over 60 years.

Country: Austria
Date: 1939
Size: 27 ft. (17 m) long
Construction: steel
Top speed: 80 mph (130 km/h)
On board: 2 crew

GGI

Country: U.S.A.
Date: from 1935
Size: 80 ft. (25 m) long
Construction: steel
Top speed: 100 mph (160 km/h)
On board: 2 crew

GGI

American railroad companies
always built things to last, and the
streamlined *GG1* Class electrics
worked for over 50 years. Designed
by a Frenchman, they hauled 14
passenger cars and heavy freight
cars along the eastern seaboard.

Metropolitan

The Metropolitan Railway's line
north of London was one of the
first to use electric power for its
passenger trains. Faster than
steam, 20 of these locomotives
were built. They were named after
famous people such as Florence
Nightingale and Sir Christopher
Wren. Two of the
engines survive
in museums.

Country: Britain
Date: from 1904
Size: 40 ft. (12 m) long
Construction: steel
Top speed: 65 mph (105 km/h)
On board: 2 crew

Metropolitan

CC7102

In March 1955, SNCF (the French Railways) wanted to see just how fast an electric locomotive could safely go. It chose a plain working train (*CC7102*) and another (*BB9004*) for tests. Each train was fitted with a streamlined front end to improve wind resistance. The engines both reached a still unbeaten record speed of 205½ mph (331.5 km/h).

Country: France
Date: 1952
Size: 62 ft. (19 m) long
Construction: steel
Top speed: 87 mph (140 km/h) on standard working models
On board: 2 crew

CC7102

Class 101

The latest German electric locomotives are giants. They can haul 2,500-ton freight trains at 100 mph (150 km/h), or 14 passenger cars. It is common for them to travel 1,000 mi. (1,600 km) in a single day. The locomotive is filled with computer-controls and can be started in a few seconds. A control center warns the driver of hazards.

Country: Germany
Date: from 1996
Size: 62 ft. (19 m) long
Construction: steel
Top speed: 135 mph (220 km/h)
On board: 2 crew

Class 101

Gatwick Express

These new passenger trains are nicknamed "Darth Vaders" because their odd-looking front ends look like something out of a *Star Wars* movie. They carry up to 365 passengers at short intervals between London's Victoria Station and Gatwick Airport. Four coaches in each eight-car train are fitted with electric motors which pick up current from a 750-volt third rail along the normal tracks.

Country: Britain
Date: 1999
Size: 520 ft. (160 m) long
Construction: steel
Top speed: 100 mph (160 km/h)
On board: 2 crew

Gatwick Express

TEE Express (Europe)

Pendolino (Italy)

Bullet Train (Japan)

Eurostar (France/Britain)

ICE (Germany)

Express types

High-speed express trains tend to have a smooth, slanting, or bullet-shaped nose and streamlined cars. They can be powered by diesel engines positioned behind the driver's cab, or by electricity drawn from overhead cables.

High-speed Trains

High-speed trains are vital for the future of railroads. The *TGV*, *ICE*, *Eurostar*, Japanese *Bullet Train*, and other super-express trains have won back many passengers who normally travel long distances between major cities by air. Cruising speeds of 155 mph (250 km/h) and higher have cut train journey times, while improved track, suspension systems, and soundproofing give a more comfortable ride. In the next 20 years, trains will regularly run at 300 mph (500 km/h)—10 times faster than the first trains.

Large seats and windows, and carpeted corridors, make the interior of a high-speed train comfortable and relaxing. There are tables at most seats, often grouped in fours for business people or families.

Driver's cab

Streamlined shape

Headlights

Driver's door

Wheels

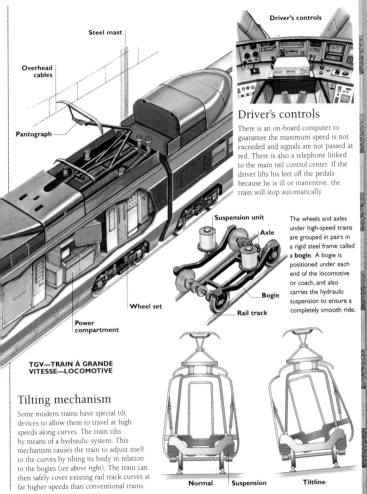

Steel mast

Overhead cables

Pantograph

Driver's controls

Driver's controls

There is an on-board computer to guarantee the maximum speed is not exceeded and signals are not passed at red. There is also a telephone linked to the main rail control center. If the driver lifts his feet off the pedals because he is ill or inattentive, the train will stop automatically.

Suspension unit

Axle

Bogie

Rail track

The wheels and axles under high-speed trains are grouped in pairs in a rigid steel frame called a **bogie**. A bogie is positioned under each end of the locomotive or coach, and also carries the hydraulic suspension to ensure a completely smooth ride.

Wheel set

Power compartment

TGV—TRAIN À GRANDE VITESSE—LOCOMOTIVE

Tilting mechanism

Some modern trains have special tilt devices to allow them to travel at high speeds along curves. The train tilts by means of a hydraulic system. This mechanism causes the train to adjust itself to the curves by tilting its body in relation to the bogies (*see above right*). The train can then safely cover existing rail track curves at far higher speeds than conventional trains.

Normal   **Suspension**   **Tiltline**

87

Around the World on Rail

By the end of World War I (1914–18), there were about 1 million mi. (1.6 million km) of rail routes, a quarter of which were in the United States. Rail had become the most widely used machine-assisted transportation around the world. Great engineering feats of the 20th century, such as the Trans-Siberian Railroad, are still heavily used today, while many modern trains can carry 1,000 passengers or haul thousands of tons of freight cargo across continents.

Robinson 2-8-0

Hundreds of these cheap but strong British freight steam engines were exported all over the world to move supplies and soldiers during wars. They were camouflaged to make them harder to spot by enemy planes.

Robinson 2-8-0

Country: Britain
Date: 1914
Size: 62 ft. (19 m) long
Construction: steel
Top speed: 60 mph (100 km/h)
On board: 2 crew

Country: Britain
Date: 1923
Size: 70 ft. (22 m) long
Construction: steel
Top speed: 100 mph (160 km/h)
On board: 2 crew

Flying Scotsman

Flying Scotsman

One of the powerful Pacific Class locomotives, *Flying Scotsman* was built to haul the fastest non-stop London-Edinburgh expresses. Water was scooped up from special troughs in the track so it would not have to stop. Over a 40-year period it covered over 3 million mi. (4.75 million km). When it was replaced by diesels, the locomotive was rescued from the scrapyard and restored to full working order. It remains one of the most famous locomotives ever built.

Pullman

American George Mortimer Pullman (1831–97) built luxury passenger coaches that today are known as *Pullmans*. Railway companies paid to use these carriages as early as 1875, and the British *Brighton Belle* electric trains used them until 1972. Many of these hotels-on-wheels have been restored for the *Orient Express* service run by VSOE (Venice Simplon Orient Express).

Pullman

Country: worldwide
Date: 1932
Size: 320 ft. (100 m) long
Construction: steel
Top speed: 90 mph (145 km/h)
On board: 152 passengers

Trans-Siberian

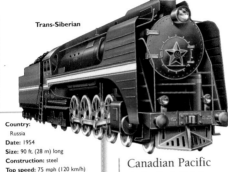

Trans-Siberian

The *Trans-Siberian Express* takes nine days to travel the 5,777 mi. (9,297 km) between Moscow and Vladivostock, making it the world's longest single train journey. The line was completed in 1905 and was then the world's most northerly track. Today it uses electric, diesel, and steam trains.

Country:
Russia
Date: 1954
Size: 90 ft. (28 m) long
Construction: steel
Top speed: 75 mph (120 km/h)
On board: 2 crew

Canadian Pacific

The Canadian Pacific Railway (renamed Canadian National) runs from the east to the west coast of Canada. Passenger trains take three days to cover the 2,880-mi. (4,634-km) journey from Montreal to Vancouver. They are often over 20 cars long, and run past lakes and through prairie country before making the steep climb into the Rocky Mountains.

Country: Canada
Date: 1955
Size: 1,600 ft. (1,000 m) long
Construction: steel
Top speed: 65 mph (100 km/h)
On board: 700 passengers

Canadian Pacific

Blue Train

South Africa has two *Blue Trains* for its 1,000 mi. (1,600 km) journey from Pretoria to Cape Town (some also go to Victoria Falls). They have 18 carriages offering the world's most luxurious passenger service with private bedrooms and bathrooms.

Country: South Africa
Date: 1972
Size: 1,000 ft. (620 m) long
Construction: steel
Top speed: 50 mph (80 km/h)
On board: 100 passengers

Blue Train

Australian long haul

The Hammersley Iron Company runs freight trains with up to 210 wagons, each loaded with over 100 tons of ore. Three locomotives are needed to get them moving. Along the route is the world's longest continuous stretch of straight track—297 mi. (478 km) across the Australian Nullabor Plain.

Australian long haul

Country: Australia
Date: 1980s
Size: ½ mi. (1 km) long
Construction: steel
Top speed: 55 mph (90 km/h)
On board: 2 crew

Carrying Goods by Rail

In the days before huge semis and trailer rigs, lots of smaller trains carried all sorts of smaller goods. Today, goods carried by rail tend to be bulk items such as coal or sand in open cars, or liquefied gas carried in insulated tankers. Large manufactured products such as cars are also commonly transported by freight trains usually on double-tier cars.

Caboose

Old-style coal car

Country: Britain
Date: 1949
Size: 27 ft. (8 m) long
Construction: steel, wood
Top speed: 65 mph (100 km/h)
Number built: 1,250
On board: 1 brakeman

Caboose

Freight trains used to have cars in which the brakeman sat in a special wooden observation car coupled to the end of the freight cars. His job was to keep an eye on cars whose brakes were sticking, or even spilling their load.

Old-style coal car

Railroads once made far more money transporting coal than carrying passengers. Coal was loaded into wagons with simple wooden sides, no roof, and primitive brakes. Sometimes 50 wagons were made up into one train.

Country: worldwide
Date: from 1850
Size: 16 ft. (5 m) long
Construction: steel, wood
Top speed: 50 mph (80 km/h)
Number built: millions
On board: 0

Merry-go-round

Modern coal-fired power stations are fed by a train named a *merry-go-round*—so called because the train never stops moving. As it travels slowly past the unloading area, a lever opens a door on the bottom of each wagon to release the coal straight onto a conveyor belt and into the furnace.

Country: Britain
Date: from 1929
Size: 60 ft. (18 m) long
Construction: steel
Top speed: 75 mph (50 km/h)
Number built: 68
On board: 20 sorters

Traveling post office

Merry-go-round

Country: Britain
Date: 1965
Size: 20 ft. (6 m) long
Construction: steel
Top speed: 50 mph (75 km/h)
Number built: over 1,000
On board: 2 crew

Traveling post office

Postmen used to travel on mail trains to sort letters and packages before they arrived at their destination. Bags of mail waiting to be sorted were hung on a large net attached to a steel frame on the side of the track and snatched into the train at high speed.

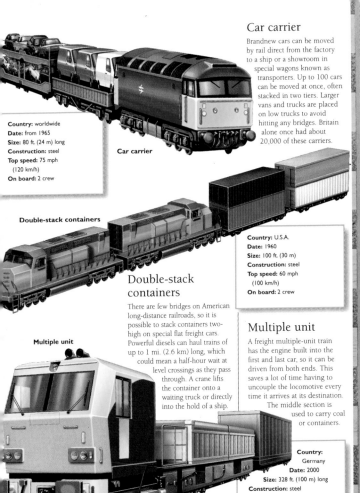

Car carrier

Brandnew cars can be moved by rail direct from the factory to a ship or a showroom in special wagons known as transporters. Up to 100 cars can be moved at once, often stacked in two tiers. Larger vans and trucks are placed on low trucks to avoid hitting any bridges. Britain alone once had about 20,000 of these carriers.

Country: worldwide
Date: from 1965
Size: 80 ft. (24 m) long
Construction: steel
Top speed: 75 mph (120 km/h)
On board: 2 crew

Car carrier

Double-stack containers

Double-stack containers

There are few bridges on American long-distance railroads, so it is possible to stack containers two-high on special flat freight cars. Powerful diesels can haul trains of up to 1 mi. (2.6 km) long, which could mean a half-hour wait at level crossings as they pass through. A crane lifts the container onto a waiting truck or directly into the hold of a ship.

Country: U.S.A.
Date: 1960
Size: 100 ft. (30 m)
Construction: steel
Top speed: 60 mph (100 km/h)
On board: 2 crew

Multiple unit

A freight multiple-unit train has the engine built into the first and last car, so it can be driven from both ends. This saves a lot of time having to uncouple the locomotive every time it arrives at its destination. The middle section is used to carry coal or containers.

Multiple unit

Country: Germany
Date: 2000
Size: 328 ft. (100 m) long
Construction: steel
Top speed: 75 mph (120 km/h)
On board: 2 crew

Traveling Underground

Big cities need public transportation to move large numbers of people around, and often this system is hidden underground to keep travelers away from roads and save valuable building space. Up to 50,000 people can be moved in one direction every hour, at speeds of 10–50 mph (16 to 80 km/h) and often without the delays transportation has above ground. Most underground trains are electric and get their power from a third rail. The first underground railroad was built in London in 1863.

Country: Britain
Date: 1866
Size: 33 ft. (10 m) long
Construction: steel
Top speed: 50 mph (80 km/h)
On board: 2 crew

Metropolitan No. 23

Metropolitan No. 23

Although it is now all-electric, the London Underground started with steam. To stop smoke from filling the tunnels and choking the passengers, large pipes were fitted to the side of these locomotives to divert the smoke into water tanks. In the early days, the driver did not have the luxury of a roof over his head. This locomotive can be seen today at the London Transport Museum.

Country: France
Date: from 1960
Size: 66 ft. (20 m) long
Construction: steel, aluminum
Top speed: 35 mph (55 km/h)
On board: 80 per car

Paris Metro

Country: U.S.A.
Date: from 1950
Size: 75 ft. (23 m) long
Construction: steel
Top speed: 50 mph (80 km/h)
On board: 80 per car

New York subway

With 25 separate lines and 469 stations, the New York subway is one of the busiest in the world. Over 1,000 million people a year buy a subway ticket. Most of the famous old trains, which were noisy, shabby, uncomfortable, and plastered with graffiti, are being replaced by new stock.

Paris Metro

Over 260 mi. (400 km) of rail track threads its way underneath France's capital city, serving over 450 stations. The trains make very little noise because they have rubber tires (making the ride much more comfortable than riding on steel wheels). Over 1,500 million passengers a year ride on the *Paris Metro* with over 4,500 cars in daily service.

New York subway

Country: Britain
Date: from 1977
Size: 42 ft. (13 m) long
Construction: steel
Top speed: 34 mph (54 km/h)
On board: 36 per car

"Clockwork Orange"

Trains on the Glasgow Underground are nicknamed "Clockwork Oranges" because of their bright color (and after a well-known novel and film of the same name). Formed of several cars coupled together, they run in a circle under the city center, going under the River Clyde twice.

Hong Kong Metro

Millions of tons of earth had to be moved to make room for the new fully automatic section of this metro linking the island city to its modern Chinese airport. A seven-car metro leaves the airport platform every three minutes.

Country: China
Date: 1998
Size: 42 ft. (13 m) long
Construction: steel, aluminum
Top speed: 85 mph (125 km/h)
On board: 60 per car

Hong Kong Metro

Country: China
Date: 1998
Size: 42 ft. (13 m) long
Construction: steel
Top speed: 50 mph (80 km/h)
On board: 100 per car

"Clockwork Orange"

Country: U.S.A.
Date: 1972
Size: 75 ft. (23 m) long
Construction: steel
Top speed: 50 mph (80 km/h)
On board: 100

San Francisco BART

San Francisco BART

There are 700 fully automatic BART (Bay Area Rapid Transit) trains running on special wide tracks around San Francisco, California. They have a strange lopsided, one-eyed appearance because the driver only has one front window. The 3½-mi. (5.8-km) tunnel to Oakland is the longest underwater rail tunnel in the U.S.

Guangzhou Metro

Despite being the third largest city in China, Guangzhou did not get a metro system until 1998. Space-age trains now glide alongside gleaming new skyscrapers and then past the old-fashioned wooden houses. Although there are only 16 stations at present, there could be hundreds before the end of the decade. The coaches were built in Berlin, Germany, and sent to China by ship.

Guangzhou Metro

Hong Kong Metro

Light Rail

"Light rail" vehicles are simply modern versions of old-fashioned trams. Like metros (see pages 92–93), they can move thousands of people through the streets very quickly. Because they run mainly on electricity, they do not cause the same pollution as cars and buses. While they are expensive to build, they can last five times as long as conventional systems before they need to be replaced. Fully automatic systems are also more common, as with London's Docklands Light Railway.

Old London tram

Country: Britain
Date: from 1900
Size: 36 ft. (11 m) long
Construction: steel, wood
Top speed: 30 mph (50 km/h)
On board: 55 passengers

European tram

Country: Germany
Date: 1960
Size: 40 ft. (25 m) long
Construction: steel
Top speed: 40 mph (65 km/h)
On board: 150+ passengers

European tram

There are over 20,000 of these trams on German and other European streets. Power comes from overhead cables laid out parallel to the rails. The rails have priority over road users, which helps reduce traffic jams. Also, because no fuel is carried, there is less pollution in city centers. Trams can run for 50 years without replacement, so all in all they offer a welcome alternative means of public transportation.

Old London tram

Double-decker trams running on sunken rails were once a common sight in cities, first towed by horses and later driven by electric power. The driver was often exposed to the rain. The decision to scrap trams after the motor bus became established in the 1920s is now seen as a big mistake, because they were better for the environment than conventional fuel engines.

New York airtrain

Kennedy Airport's new airtrain will cut the journey times into New York city center from 45 to just 12 minutes. Built of steel and running past 10 elevated stations, New York's Airtrain for 2002 will run on a raised steel track at speeds of up to 68 mph (110 km/h) driven by powerful electric motors. It is also designed to run without a driver.

New York airtrain

Country: U.S.A.
Date: 2002
Size: 50 ft. (15 m)
Construction: steel, aluminum
Top speed: 70 mph (110 km/h)
On board: 100 passengers

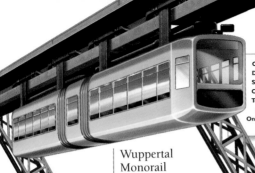

Country: Germany
Date: from 1972
Size: 78 ft. (24 m) long
Construction: steel
Top speed: 25 mph
(40 km/h)
On board: 40 passengers

Wuppertal Monorail

Wuppertal Monorail

Although it looks like a carnival ride, the suspended cars rattling under the green girders high above the River Wupper in Germany are used by thousands of people every day. People traveling on this rather special system get a unique view of the towns of Barmen or Elberfield below.

Lille VAL

The French city of Lille was the first in the world to get a fully automatic metro. There is no driver, and except for the passengers, the only person on board is the ticket inspector. The electric train wheels have rubber tires. *VAL* has been so successful that extensions are being built in all directions.

Country: France
Date: from 1983
Size: 85 ft. (26 m) long
Construction: steel, aluminum
Top speed: 50 mph (80 km/h)
On board: 50 passengers

Lille VAL

Country: Germany
Date: from 1995
Size: 81 ft. (25 m) long
Construction: steel
Top speed: 62 mph
(100 km/h)
On board: 75 passengers

Regio-Sprinter

The *Regio-Sprinter* is one of several trams that can go long distances over normal rail tracks. Powered by a diesel engine instead of electricity, it is very cheap to run. The doors are so close to the ground that there is no need to build a special high platform.

Regio-Sprinter

Running on Empty

With fuel supplies dwindling and cities getting more polluted from vehicle exhaust emissions, the search is on for forms of transportation that use less fossil fuel energy. Car makers have produced "hybrid" cars that run on both electricity and gasoline. The power of the sun could offer another solution, and there are already some exciting experimental cars and boats. Future cars may even be powered by hydrogen.

When fog and pollutants, such as exhaust fumes, get mixed up in cities, they create **smog**. This damages health and the atmosphere.

This Norwegian **TH!NK** electric car runs on batteries that need recharging after about 53 mi. (85 km). The top speed is 90 km/h (56 mph). The two-seater, which has a plastic body and aluminum frame has no exhaust and does not rust.

This 68-ft. (21-m) catamaran, called **Solar Sailor**, combines wind and solar power. It has eight large, winglike solar panels, which also work as sails. It is based in Sydney Harbor, where it travels at 12 mph (20 km/h) and can carry up to 110 passengers.

Using strong magnetic forces, a **Maglev train** is able to hover a few millimeters above the tracks. There is therefore no friction between the train and the track, which means the trains can go faster while using less energy. *Maglev* (short for magnetic levitation) trains are being developed in Japan and Germany, where experts predict that they will run at speeds of up to 435 mph (700 km/h).

The fastest solar-powered car in the world is **Honda's Dream**. It can cruise at 56 mph (90 km/h) on solar power, and reaches 90 mph (145 km/h) with battery power added. In 1996 it crossed Australia, covering 1,870 mi. (3,009 km) in 33 hours and 32 minutes—a record.

In the Air

*For thousands of years, people watched the birds'
mastery of the air and dreamed of joining them.
The first people to fly used balloons that blew where
the wind took them. Then, at the beginning of the
20th century, the Wright Brothers learned the secret
of powered flight. These early adventures led to
today's air transport industry and military air forces.*

*Look up into a clear blue sky and you may see a tiny
speck streaking through the air. It is probably an
airliner flying at almost 600 mph (1,000 km/h),
6 mi. (10 km) above the Earth. It may
not return to the ground for another
8,000 mi. (13,000 km). There are more types
of aircraft flying today than ever
before—from hang gliders and zepplins
to airplanes and supersonic jets.*

Blériot XI monoplane

A **Boeing 747-400** is nearly 2,000 times
heavier than the **Blériot XI monoplane**
(*above*), which made the first airplane flight
across the English Channel in 1909.

99

What is a plane?

A typical plane has a long slender fuselage (body), with a wing on each side. The tail has a vertical fin (vertical stabilizer) and tail (horizontal stabilizer). There is an engine in front, or two or more engines attached to its wings or mounted on its tail. Wheels may fold up and into the nose and wings after takeoff.

Gossamer Penguin was a solar-powered aircraft designed by Dr. Paul MacCready and initially flown by his son, who was 13 and weighed about 80 lb (36 kg). The plane itself only weighed 65 lb (30 kg)! The first test flight was in 1980. The first official flight flown by Janice Brown traveled just over 2 mi. (3 km) in 14 minutes and 21 seconds and used solar power directly.

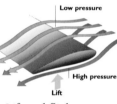

Low pressure

High pressure

Lift

Lift and flight

Planes fly because of the shape of their wings. Air flowing over the curved top speeds up and has a lower pressure than air passing underneath.

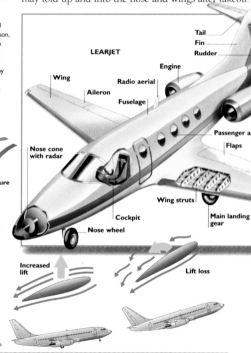

LEARJET

Tail
Fin
Rudder
Engine
Radio aerial
Wing
Aileron
Fuselage
Passenger ar
Flaps
Nose cone with radar
Wing struts
Main landing gear
Cockpit
Nose wheel

Lift

Increased lift

Lift loss

1. As a plane starts moving, its wings cut through the air and create lift.

2. When its nose tips up, tilting the wings, they create even more lift.

3. But if a wing tilts too much, the air above it breaks up and it loses lift.

Ferrari 250 GTO

Country: Italy
Date: 1962
Size: 14½ ft. (4.4 m) long
Body: steel
Top speed: 165 mph (266 km/h)
On board: 4

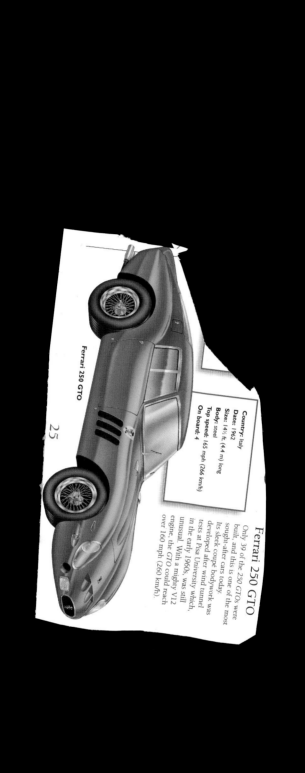

Ferrari 250 GTO

Only 39 of the 250 GTOs were built, and this is one of the most sought-after cars today. Its sleek coupé bodywork was developed after wind tunnel tests at Pisa University which, in the early 1960s, was still unusual. With a mighty V12 engine, the GTO could reach over 160 mph (260 km/h).

25

Top speed: 85 mph (136 km/h)
On board: 2 to 9

Mercedes M Class

foun...
comp...
insulati...
comfortabl...
It can also go thr...
of water without flooding...

Country: Britain
Date: 1970
Size: 14½ ft. (4.5 m) long
Body: aluminum and steel
Top speed: 100 mph (160 km/h)
On board: 5

Range Rover

Country: Germany, U.S.A.
Date: 1998
Size: 15 ft. (4.6 m) long
Body: steel
Top speed: 112 mph (180 km/h)
On board: 5 to 7

Range Rover

The large and comfortable *Range Rover* was designed as an ATV (all-terrain vehicle) to handle normal city streets or difficult muddy forest tracks. With a big V8 engine driving all four wheels, it was also powerful, so it could pull itself up steep hills or through the muddiest country.

The forces of flight

Four forces act on every airplane. Engine power thrusts it forward; air pushing back against it causes drag, trying to slow it down. Wings create lift, which acts upward, while its weight tries to pull it down.

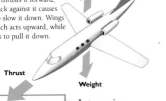

Lift

Drag

Thrust

Weight

Types of wings

The slowest aircraft are biplanes and other straight-winged airplanes. Faster planes have swept-back wings. Supersonic aircraft have triangular "delta" or diamond shaped wings. Navy planes have folding wings to fit the most planes in the smallest space. Some planes have turned-up wingtips, or winglets, to reduce drag and save fuel.

Elevator

The parts of a plane

This small plane is powered by two jet engines in its tail. The pilot steers by moving controls that tilt parts of the wings and tail. Ailerons in the wings make the plane roll, the rudder in the fin turns the nose right or left, and elevators in the tail tip the nose up or down. Flaps assist takeoff and landing.

Jet engine

Today, all but the smallest planes are powered by jet engines. These consist of several parts. A spinning fan in the front sucks in air. Some of this air is squashed in a compressor and is heated by burning fuel so that it expands and rushes out of the engine as a fast jet. The jet spins a windmill-like turbine, which drives the fan and compressor. The rest of the air flows around the engine's hot core.

Biplane

Straight wing

JET ENGINE

Turbine

Exhaust jet

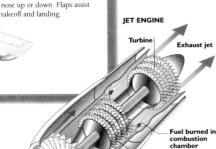

Swept-back wing

Fuel burned in combustion chamber

Compressor

Delta wing

Fan

Some air bypasses the engine's hot core

Folding wing

Air sucked in

101

The Wright Brothers

American brothers Wilbur and Orville Wright made the vital breakthrough in the search for a method of powered flight. They began by building a series of gliders, each improving on the one before. Then they designed the world's first successful powered airplane, the 1903 *Wright Flyer*. During this time they also designed and made their own engine and propellers. In 1908, Wilbur Wright took an improved version of the *Flyer* to France and dazzled Europeans with his displays of controlled flying.

Wilbur and Orville

The brothers had a prosperous business selling and manufacturing bicycles in Dayton, Ohio. Wilbur was born in 1867 and died of typhoid fever in Dayton in 1912. Orville, born in Dayton in 1871, lived until 1948. Their interest in flight was inspired by news of Otto Lilienthal's glider flights in Germany in the 1890s.

In the air!

The world's first controlled, powered airplane flight took place on the morning of December 17, 1903, at Kill Devil Hill in North Carolina. At about 10.35 A.M., a small group of local spectators who had gathered saw Orville take off, fly into the wind for 12 seconds, and land 118 ft. (36 m) away. Later the same day, Wilbur made another flight, which lasted 59 seconds and covered a distance of 850 ft. (259 m).

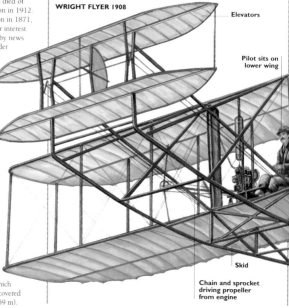

WRIGHT FLYER 1908

Elevators

Pilot sits on lower wing

Skid

Chain and sprocket driving propeller from engine

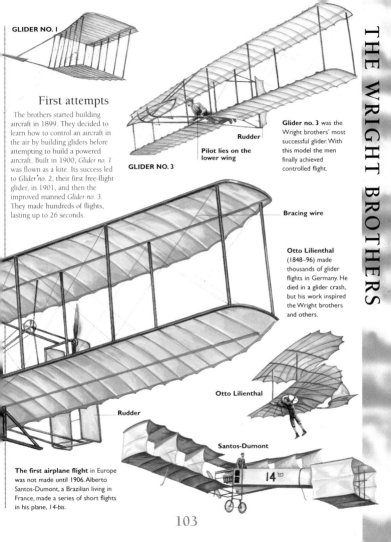

GLIDER NO. 1

First attempts

The brothers started building aircraft in 1899. They decided to learn how to control an aircraft in the air by building gliders before attempting to build a powered aircraft. Built in 1900, *Glider no. 1* was flown as a kite. Its success led to *Glider no. 2*, their first free-flight glider, in 1901, and then the improved manned *Glider no. 3*. They made hundreds of flights, lasting up to 26 seconds.

Rudder

Pilot lies on the lower wing

GLIDER NO. 3

Glider no. 3 was the Wright brothers' most successful glider. With this model the men finally achieved controlled flight.

Bracing wire

Otto Lilienthal (1848–96) made thousands of glider flights in Germany. He died in a glider crash, but his work inspired the Wright brothers and others.

Otto Lilienthal

Santos-Dumont

Rudder

The first airplane flight in Europe was not made until 1906. Alberto Santos-Dumont, a Brazilian living in France, made a series of short flights in his plane, *14-bis*.

War Planes

The first military planes were built during World War I (1914–18). They were flimsy craft—made from a wooden frame covered with fabric and powered by piston engines that drove the propellers. Their main task was to spot artillery. Fighters were built to stop the other side from doing such spying. Bombers were designed for attacking targets on the ground, and transport planes for carrying troops and supplies. Military planes today are bigger, heavier, all-metal, and jet-engined versions of these early craft.

Sopwith Camel

Probably the greatest fighter aircraft of World War I, the *Sopwith Camel* could twist and turn tightly in air fights. But it could be difficult to control, and inexperienced pilots often crashed while learning to fly it. Although known by everyone as the *Sopwith Camel*, it was actually called the *Sopwith F1*. "Camel" was a nickname that came from the hump over the twin machine guns on its nose.

Sopwith Camel

Country: Britain
Date: 1917
Size: 28 ft. (8.5 m) wingspan
Construction: wood and fabric
Top speed: 105 mph (168 km/h)
On board: 1

Boeing B-17

Boeing B-17

More than 12,000 *B-17s*, or *Flying Fortresses*, were built during World War II (1939–45). It was a long-range daylight heavy bomber. It could climb to over 33,000 ft. (10,000 m)—as high as modern jet airliners—and its fuel tanks could take it 1,100 mi. (1,700 km). The *B-17* carried up to 6,000 lb (2,700 kg) of bombs, and was also armed with up to 13 machine guns to fight off attacks from enemy planes.

Country: U.S.A.
Date: 1935
Size: 104 ft. (32 m) wingspan
Construction: armored alloy
Top speed: 287 mph (462 km/h)
On board: 10

North American Aviation P-51 Mustang

The *P-51 Mustang* was the best all-around fighter of World War II (1939–45). It was a combination of American air frame with a British Rolls-Royce Merlin engine. More than 15,000 *Mustangs* were built during the war. They were armed with six machine guns and carried up to 2,000 lb (900 kg) of bombs and extra fuel tanks.

North American Aviation P-51 Mustang

Country: U.S.A.
Date: 1940
Size: 37 ft. (11.3 m) wingspan
Construction: lightweight alloy
Top speed: 437 mph (703 km/h)
On board: 1

Boeing B-52 Stratofortress

A giant among bombers, the *B-52* is still in service. It can carry over 50,000 lb (22,700 kg) of bombs and missiles. It has a range of over 10,000 mi. (16,000 km)—half way around the world. Remote-controlled machine guns in its tail fight off attacks.

Boeing B-52 Stratofortress

Country: U.S.A.
Date: 1952
Size: 185 ft. (56 m) wingspan
Construction: armored alloy
Top speed: 595 mph (958 km/h)
On board: 6

British Aerospace Harrier Jet

British Aerospace Harrier Jet

The *Harrier* was the first VTOL (vertical take-off and landing) combat plane. Its engine nozzles swivel so the jets from the engine can be pointed downward for takeoff, and then can be swung backward for flying. It made its combat debut in the Falklands War (1982), where *Harriers* operated from aircraft carriers and the decks of cargo ships.

Country: Britain
Date: 1966
Size: 30 ft. (9 m) wingspan
Construction: lightweight alloy
Top speed: 660 mph (1,065 km/h)
On board: 1

F-15 Eagle

This is a long-range fighter that can also be used as a bomber and ground attack aircraft. Its two side-by-side jet engines can power it to two and half times the speed of sound, and it can climb to 60,000 ft. (18,000 m).

F-15 Eagle

Country: U.S.A.
Date: 1972
Size: 42 ft. (13 m) wingspan
Construction: lightweight alloy
Top speed: 1,675 mph (2,700 km/h)
On board: 2

Lockheed F-117 Nighthawk

Better known as the *Stealth Fighter*, the *F-117* attacks ground targets with pinpoint accuracy. It uses laser-guided bombs stored in its weapons bays. Its shape and black coating make it almost invisible on enemy radar.

Country: U.S.A.
Date: 1981
Size: 43 ft. (13.5 m) wingspan
Construction: alloy and composites
Top speed: 645 mph (1,040 km/h)
On board: 1

Lockheed F-117 Nighthawk

Commercial Planes

In the 1930s, the first propeller planes flew their passengers slow and low, because piston engines were not very powerful. Flying boats also took wealthy people across continents. From the 1960s, jet aircraft flew higher and faster, and were affordable for vacationers. The biggest airplane is the Boeing 747-400, which can carry 568 passengers. It is flown by a crew of only two, since computers have now replaced the flight engineer.

Boeing 247

Lockheed Constellation

Country:
  U.S.A.
Date: 1933
Size: 74 ft. (22.6 m) wingspan
Body: lightweight alloy
Top speed: 189 mph (304 km/h)
On board: 2 crew, 10 passengers

Boeing 247

The first modern commercial plane, the Boeing 247 was a streamlined all-metal plane. It had retractable wheels. It was safe and reliable because it could climb and cruise using only one of its two engines. It was designed as a mail-carrying plane, with only 10 seats for passengers.

Country: U.S.A.
Date: 1943
Size: 123 ft. (37.5 m) wingspan
Construction: lightweight alloy
Top speed: 339 mph (545 km/h)
On board: 4 crew, 81 passengers

Lockheed Constellation

Although designed as a long-range plane, the first Lockheed *Constellations* came off the assembly line during World War II, so they entered service as a military transport plane. This plane's elegant, slender shape, and comfortable, pressurized passenger cabin made it popular with airlines and passengers. Larger versions followed in the 1950s.

Country: Britain
Date: 1949
Size: 115 ft. (35 m) wingspan
Construction: lightweight alloy
Top speed: 490 mph (790 km/h)
On board: 3 crew, 44 passengers

Douglas DC-3

This airliner looks surprisingly modern for an airplane that made its first flight in 1935. More than 13,000 *DC-3s* were built. It was so successful that by 1938 most American air travelers flew in *DC-3s*. It served as a transporter during World War II and returned to airline service after the war. Remarkably, in 1999 about 200 *DC-3s* were still in civil and military service.

De Havilland Comet

Douglas DC-3

Country: U.S.A.
Date: 1935
Size: 95 ft. (29 m) wingspan
Construction: lightweight alloy
Top speed: 185 mph (298 km/h)
On board: 2 crew, 21 passengers

De Havilland Comet

The *Comet* was the world's first jet plane. Passengers loved it because it flew higher and faster than any other plane. However, it suffered a weakness in its metal skin that allowed it to crack. It was completely re-designed and flew again on transatlantic routes as the larger *Comet 4*. But by then, Boeing's bigger and faster 707 was flying.

Boeing 747-100

Boeing 747-100

The 747 "Jumbo Jet" began as a design for a military transporter, which Boeing changed into an airliner. Powered by four turbofan engines, it was the biggest airplane and the first of a new type, called a wide-bodied jet. The 747's passenger cabin has an an upper deck and a first-class lounge.

Country: U.S.A.
Date: 1969
Size: 196 ft. (59.6 m) wingspan
Construction: lightweight alloy
Top speed: 640 mph (1,030 km/h)
On board: 3 crew, 490 passengers

BAC/Aerospatiale Concorde

Concorde is the only supersonic commercial jet: it can fly at Mach 2 (twice the speed of sound). It is 204-ft. (62.1-m) long and cruises at 60,000 ft. (18,000 m). It can fly from London to New York in just three and a half hours. *Concorde* started as two supersonic projects being studied in France and Britain. Although it was a great technical success, its future came into question when an Air France *Concorde* crashed on take-off in Paris in July 2000.

BAC/Aerospatiale Concorde

Country: Britain, France
Date: 1969
Size: 84 ft. (25.6 m) wingspan
Construction: lightweight alloy
Top speed: 1,450 mph (2,333 km/h)
On board: 3 crew, 144 passengers

Airbus 340

The *A340* is the latest in the series of European Airbus airliners that started with the *A300* in 1972. It is Europe's biggest airliner and the first four-engine Airbus. It also has the longest range of all the Airbuses, 7,600 mi. (12,225 km). In 1993, an *A340* set several distance records when it flew around the world from Paris, making only one landing, in New Zealand. It is a rival to the Boeing 747 (*see above*).

Airbus 340

Country: Europe
Date: 1991
Size: 74 ft. (60.3 m) wingspan
Construction: lightweight alloy
Top speed: 553 mph (890 km/h)
On board: 2 crew, 440 passengers

Light Aircraft

Light aircraft are small planes with many uses, such as pilot training, crop spraying, and aerial photography. Most are flown for business and pleasure. A great deal of leisure flying is done in gliders, soaring into the sky on rising air currents. Hang gliders, where the pilot hangs underneath a kitelike wing, also use these rising "thermals" to stay airborne. Microlights are for one or two people: a three-axis microlight is steered by a control stick and pedals like larger aircraft, while a flexwing is steered by moving a bar attached to the wing.

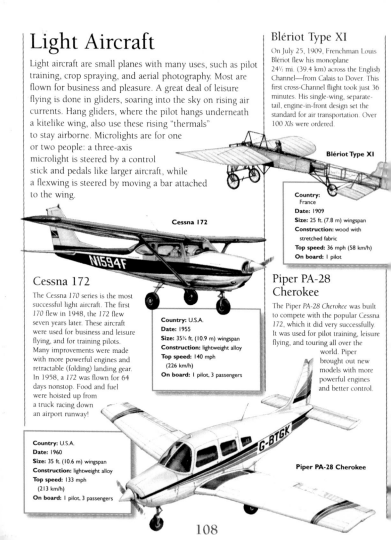

Blériot Type XI

On July 25, 1909, Frenchman Louis Blériot flew his monoplane 24½ mi. (39.4 km) across the English Channel—from Calais to Dover. This first cross-Channel flight took just 36 minutes. His single-wing, separate-tail, engine-in-front design set the standard for air transportation. Over 100 XIs were ordered.

Blériot Type XI

> **Country:** France
> **Date:** 1909
> **Size:** 25 ft. (7.8 m) wingspan
> **Construction:** wood with stretched fabric
> **Top speed:** 36 mph (58 km/h)
> **On board:** 1 pilot

Cessna 172

Cessna 172

The Cessna 170 series is the most successful light aircraft. The first 170 flew in 1948, the 172 flew seven years later. These aircraft were used for business and leisure flying, and for training pilots. Many improvements were made with more powerful engines and retractable (folding) landing gear. In 1958, a 172 was flown for 64 days nonstop. Food and fuel were hoisted up from a truck racing down an airport runway!

> **Country:** U.S.A.
> **Date:** 1955
> **Size:** 35¼ ft. (10.9 m) wingspan
> **Construction:** lightweight alloy
> **Top speed:** 140 mph (226 km/h)
> **On board:** 1 pilot, 3 passengers

Piper PA-28 Cherokee

The Piper PA-28 Cherokee was built to compete with the popular Cessna 172, which it did very successfully. It was used for pilot training, leisure flying, and touring all over the world. Piper brought out new models with more powerful engines and better control.

> **Country:** U.S.A.
> **Date:** 1960
> **Size:** 35 ft. (10.6 m) wingspan
> **Construction:** lightweight alloy
> **Top speed:** 133 mph (213 km/h)
> **On board:** 1 pilot, 3 passengers

Piper PA-28 Cherokee

Learjet

The *Learjet* is the classic business jet. It was named after William P. Lear, who developed the design. The first *Learjet* was an instant success because of its good looks, reasonable price, and high speed. Because of its small size, light weight, and the power of its twin jet engines, it could climb faster than a fighter. Further versions were built, increasing its range from 1,584 mi. (2,549 km) to 3,155 mi. (5,078 km) and its passenger-carrying capacity from five to nine.

Learjet

Country: U.S.A.
Date: 1963
Size: 35½ ft. (10.8 m) wingspan
Construction: lightweight alloy
Top speed: 549 mph (884 kmh)
On board: 2 crew, 5 passengers

Duo Discus Glider

Country: Germany
Date: 1993
Size: 65½ ft. (20 m) wingspan
Construction: fiberglass
Top speed: 155 mph (250 km/h)
On board: 2

Duo Discus Glider

From 1985 to 1995, the *Discus* won six world gliding championships. To save weight, its slender body and swept-back wings are made from fiberglass and foam plastic. The slightly larger two-seater *Duo* model is based on this successful single-seater and is used for training.

Country: Britain
Date: 1993
Size: 30¾ ft. (9.4 m) wingspan
Construction: composite frame
Top speed: 50 mph (80 kmh)
On board: 1 pilot

Flexwing Microlight

The *Quantum 912 Flexwing* is a weight-shift microlight, steered by moving a bar attached to the wing. It can carry a pilot and passenger with a combined weight of up to 375 lb (172 kg). Fully loaded, it can climb at 1,200 ft. (365 m) per minute.

Pegasus Breeze

Flexwing Microlight

Pegasus Breeze

This hang-glider was first developed from a kitelike wing as a NASA project designed by Dr. Francis Rogallo to land U.S. spacecraft back on Earth. However, it was never used for that, and instead, was developed for the new sport of hang gliding. Weighing only 61½ lb (28 kg), it has a semi-rigid wing with material stretched over a frame.

Country: Britain
Date: 1995
Size: 34 ft. (10.35 m) wingspan
Construction: alloy and composites
Top speed: 88 mph (140 km/h)
On board: 1 to 2

Helicopters

The first helicopter flight was in 1907. It took another 30 years to develop the first practical helicopter, the *Vought-Sikorsky VS-300*, because of formidable technical problems. Once these were solved, helicopters progressed rapidly. Until the 1950s, the rotors (blades) of early helicopters were powered by piston engines. Then more powerful turboshaft ("jet"-type) engines became available. From air-sea rescue to police surveillance, helicopters are highly versatile machines.

Sikorsky R-4

Country: U.S.A.
Date: 1942
Size: 38-ft. (11.6-m) rotors
Construction: fabric and aluminum alloy
Top speed: 81 mph (131 km/h)
On board: 1 crew, 1 passenger

Sikorsky R-4

Sikorsky transformed his experimental *VS-300* (*see below*) into a production model, the *R-4*, by covering it with fabric and giving it an enclosed cockpit. Its simple layout and easy maintenance made it a popular military helicopter.

Breguet-Richet No. 1

Breguet-Richet No. 1

On September 29, 1907, in Douai, France, the *Breguet-Richet No. 1* became the first man-carrying helicopter to leave the ground. The lift was created by four rotors driven by a 50-horsepower Antoinette engine. The ungainly craft was very unstable and had to be steadied by four men with poles.

Country: France
Date: 1907
Size: four 26¼-ft. (8-m) rotors
Construction: wood and metal frame
Top speed: zero (hovered only)
On board: 1 crew

Country: U.S.A.
Date: 1961
Size: 60-ft. (18.3-m) rotors
Construction: aluminum alloy
Top speed: 160 mph (256 km/h)
On board: 2 crew, 55 passengers

CH-47 Chinook

Vought-Sikorsky

Vought-Sikorsky

The modern helicopter, with a large overhead rotor and small tail rotor to balance the twisting effect of the main rotor, was developed in the 1930s by Igor Sikorsky. His *VS-300* lifted off for the first time on September 14, 1939, and made its first untethered flight on May 13, 1940.

Country: U.S.A.
Date: 1939
Size: 38-ft. (11.6-m) rotors
Construction: tubular metal frame
Top speed: unknown
On board: 1 crew

CH-47 Chinook

The *Chinook* was developed to meet the U.S. Army's need for an all-weather transport helicopter. The current model, the *CH-47D*, can carry 55 men and 10 tons of cargo slung underneath it or 6 tons inside.

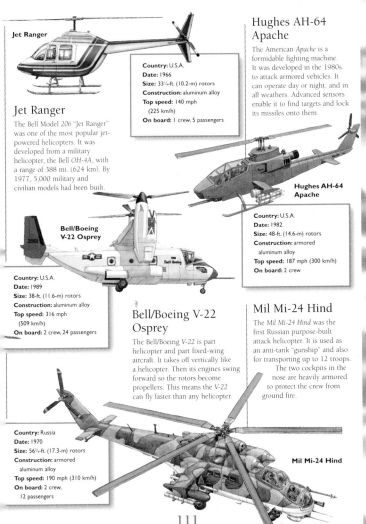

Jet Ranger

Jet Ranger

The Bell Model *206* "Jet Ranger" was one of the most popular jet-powered helicopters. It was developed from a military helicopter, the Bell *OH-4A*, with a range of 388 mi. (624 km). By 1977, 5,000 military and civilian models had been built.

Country: U.S.A.
Date: 1966
Size: 33¼-ft. (10.2-m) rotors
Construction: aluminum alloy
Top speed: 140 mph (225 km/h)
On board: 1 crew, 5 passengers

Hughes AH-64 Apache

The American *Apache* is a formidable fighting machine. It was developed in the 1980s to attack armored vehicles. It can operate day or night, and in all weathers. Advanced sensors enable it to find targets and lock its missiles onto them.

Hughes AH-64 Apache

Country: U.S.A.
Date: 1982
Size: 48-ft. (14.6-m) rotors
Construction: armored aluminum alloy
Top speed: 187 mph (300 km/h)
On board: 2 crew

Bell/Boeing V-22 Osprey

Country: U.S.A.
Date: 1989
Size: 38-ft. (11.6-m) rotors
Construction: aluminum alloy
Top speed: 316 mph (509 km/h)
On board: 2 crew, 24 passengers

Bell/Boeing V-22 Osprey

The Bell/Boeing *V-22* is part helicopter and part fixed-wing aircraft. It takes off vertically like a helicopter. Then its engines swing forward so the rotors become propellers. This means the *V-22* can fly faster than any helicopter.

Mil Mi-24 Hind

The *Mil Mi-24 Hind* was the first Russian purpose-built attack helicopter. It is used as an anti-tank "gunship" and also for transporting up to 12 troops.

The two cockpits in the nose are heavily armored to protect the crew from ground fire.

Country: Russia
Date: 1970
Size: 56¾-ft. (17.3-m) rotors
Construction: armored aluminum alloy
Top speed: 190 mph (310 km/h)
On board: 2 crew, 12 passengers

Mil Mi-24 Hind

Balloons and Airships

The first people to fly were carried aloft by nothing more than a balloon, which floated upward because hot air and hydrogen gas are lighter than the surrounding cold air. Balloons would drift wherever the wind blew them, but by putting in an engine and propeller, steering was possible, and the balloon became a sausage-shaped airship or dirigible. Modern airships are filled with nonflammable helium gas.

Montgolfier Balloon

French brothers Joseph Michel and Jacques Étienne Montgolfier made the first manned flight on November, 21 1783. The air in the balloon was heated by a fire of straw. The craft drifted 5½ mi. (8 km) across Paris in 25 minutes and climbed to 1,500 ft. (450 m).

Country: France
Date: 1783
Size: 49 ft. (15 m) across
Construction: fabric
Top speed: 12½ mph (20 km/h)
On board: 2

Montgolfier Balloon

Giffard Airship

Giffard Airship

The first person to build an airship that could be steered (instead of drifting with the wind) was Henri Giffard. He hung a steam engine and propeller underneath a long, thin, hydrogen-filled balloon, so the spinning propeller pushed the craft through the air. In 1852, he flew his airship 17 mi. (27 km) from Paris to Trappes.

Country:
France
Date: 1852
Size: 144 ft. (43.9 m) long
Construction: fabric
Top speed: 5 mph (8 km/h)
On board: 1

Nulli Secundus

The British Army's first airship was completed in 1907. It was called *Dirigible number 1*, better known as *Nulli Secundus*, meaning "second to none." It was built by U.S.-born British aviator Samuel Franklin Cody.

Nulli Secundus

Country:
Britain
Date: 1907
Size: 122 ft. (37 m) long
Construction: animal skin
Top speed: 20 mph (32 km/h)
On board: 2

ZR-1 Shenandoah

The US Navy's first rigid airship was made from a lightweight metal frame with fabric stretched over it. It was also the first to be filled with helium gas instead of hydrogen, and it carried 50,000 lb (22,000 kg) of fuel and cargo.

Country: U.S.A.
Date: 1923
Size: 680 ft. (207 m) long
Construction: fabric over alloy frame
Top speed: 81 mph (130 km/h)
On board: 43 (on last flight)

ZR-1 Shenandoah

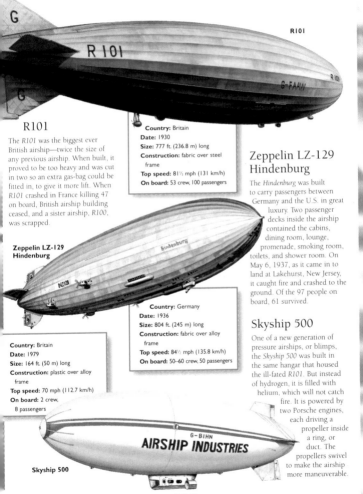

R101

The *R101* was the biggest ever British airship—twice the size of any previous airship. When built, it proved to be too heavy and was cut in two so an extra gas-bag could be fitted in, to give it more lift. When *R101* crashed in France killing 47 on board, British airship building ceased, and a sister airship, *R100*, was scrapped.

Country: Britain
Date: 1930
Size: 777 ft. (236.8 m) long
Construction: fabric over steel frame
Top speed: 81½ mph (131 km/h)
On board: 53 crew, 100 passengers

Zeppelin LZ-129 Hindenburg

Zeppelin LZ-129 Hindenburg

The *Hindenburg* was built to carry passengers between Germany and the U.S. in great luxury. Two passenger decks inside the airship contained the cabins, dining room, lounge, promenade, smoking room, toilets, and shower room. On May 6, 1937, as it came in to land at Lakehurst, New Jersey, it caught fire and crashed to the ground. Of the 97 people on board, 61 survived.

Country: Germany
Date: 1936
Size: 804 ft. (245 m) long
Construction: fabric over alloy frame
Top speed: 84½ mph (135.8 km/h)
On board: 50–60 crew, 50 passengers

Skyship 500

One of a new generation of pressure airships, or blimps, the *Skyship 500* was built in the same hangar that housed the ill-fated *R101*. But instead of hydrogen, it is filled with helium, which will not catch fire. It is powered by two Porsche engines, each driving a propeller inside a ring, or duct. The propellers swivel to make the airship more maneuverable.

Country: Britain
Date: 1979
Size: 164 ft. (50 m) long
Construction: plastic over alloy frame
Top speed: 70 mph (112.7 km/h)
On board: 2 crew, 8 passengers

Skyship 500

Around-the-World Balloons

The last great aviation record of the 20th century was claimed by Bertrand Piccard and Brian Jones in 1999 when they made the first nonstop balloon flight around the world. Their historic flight in the *Breitling Orbiter 3* balloon took three weeks and covered a distance of 28,400 mi. (45,700 km) at speeds of up to 115 mph (185 km/h).

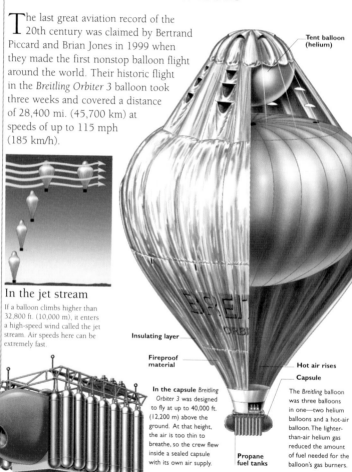

Tent balloon (helium)

In the jet stream

If a balloon climbs higher than 32,800 ft. (10,000 m), it enters a high-speed wind called the jet stream. Air speeds here can be extremely fast.

Insulating layer

Fireproof material

Hot air rises

Capsule

In the capsule *Breitling Orbiter 3* was designed to fly at up to 40,000 ft. (12,200 m) above the ground. At that height, the air is too thin to breathe, so the crew flew inside a sealed capsule with its own air supply.

Propane fuel tanks

The *Breitling* balloon was three balloons in one—two helium balloons and a hot-air balloon. The lighter-than-air helium gas reduced the amount of fuel needed for the balloon's gas burners.

114

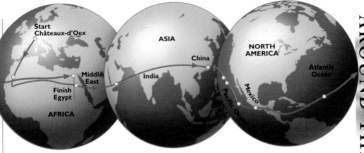

Orbiter's route

Breitling Orbiter 3 took off from Châteaux-d'Oex, Switzerland, on March 1, 1999 (*above*). It drifted south-west before finding eastward winds over North Africa. Its route took it over the Middle East, India, and China, then out across the Pacific Ocean. It crossed Mexico and set out over the Atlantic Ocean. On March 20, it crossed the finish line and landed in Egypt the next day.

Piccard Balloon

Designed by Swiss physicist Auguste Piccard, this was the first "teardrop" shaped balloon designed to accommodate the expanding gas that helped it rise. It also featured the first sealed cabin. In May 1931 it became the first balloon to ascend into the stratosphere. Piccard, with Paul Kipfer on board, reached a height of 50,135 ft. (15,281 m).

ICO Global Challenger

In December 1998, *ICO Global Challenger* carried Richard Branson, Per Lindstrand, and Steve Fossett 12,404 mi. (19,960 km) before they had to ditch in the Pacific Ocean near Hawaii.

Solo Spirit 3

Solo Spirit 3, piloted by Steve Fossett, plunged into the Coral Sea on August 16, 1998, when the balloon was torn apart by a thunderstorm. It had flown 14,236 mi. (22,900 km). Fossett was rescued from the sea the next day.

Traffic Watch

In ancient times, when there were few carts on the road or ships on the oceans, traffic looked after itself. The first traffic lights were used in Cleveland, Ohio, in 1914, and today, our heavy traffic needs even more controlling, to keep it safe and to help it run smoothly. The simple hand signals of a policeman, or a set of colored traffic lights, are still much in use to keep the roads free of congestion. However, there are also many other modern traffic systems based on computers, satellites, and radar systems to prevent air, sea, and train accidents.

Air traffic controllers guide aircraft, especially during takeoff and landing and through congested air space. They use radar to keep aircraft on precise routes called airways that keep them a safe distance from each other, and to bring them safely in to land.

Stacking is a way of dealing with aircraft as they wait to come in to land. The waiting airplanes fly in a series of ovals. Each aircraft sticks to a different altitude so they are all kept safely apart. As the first plane lands, the others move down the stack.

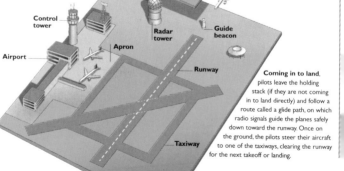

Holding stack

Glide path

Airways

Control tower

Airport

Apron

Radar tower

Guide beacon

Runway

Taxiway

Coming in to land, pilots leave the holding stack (if they are not coming in to land directly) and follow a route called a glide path, on which radio signals guide the planes safely down toward the runway. Once on the ground, the pilots steer their aircraft to one of the taxiways, clearing the runway for the next takeoff or landing.

Train signal operators use computers to control whole lengths of track and to display each train's position. Signals can be set so drivers will stop if they get too close to another train.

Tolls are used on many highways and bridges to pay for the upkeep of those routes. Vehicles stop at a booth where drivers pay to use the road. Traffic can also be counted and monitored through tolls.

Traffic police can respond quickly to any situation, dealing with traffic jams, rerouting cars in emergencies and accidents. This plastic model of a traffic policeman stands on a street in Pusan, South Korea, performing some of the same tasks as a real one.

Traffic signals may be computer-controlled, with sensors to assess the traffic flow and switch the lights to keep vehicles moving. Many traffic lights also have a button for pedestrians to press to cross the road.

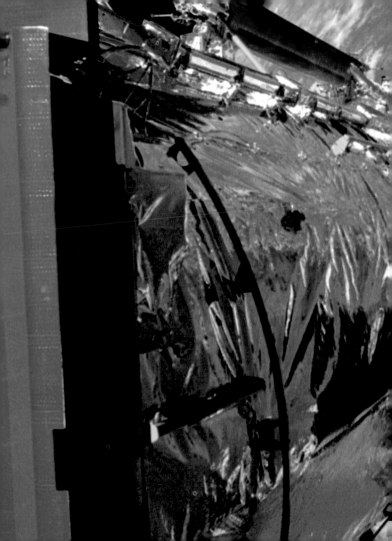

In Space

In 1961, Soviet pilot Yuri Gagarin rocketed out of the atmosphere in his Vostok capsule and orbited the Earth. His historic flight marked the beginning of manned space flight. Since then, unmanned spacecraft have explored the solar system, and people have lived in space stations and landed on the Moon. Now, space shuttles ferry people into Earth's orbit and back.

Space flight is the youngest of all the different forms of transportation, so it is not available to all of us—yet. But, just as airplanes were once flown only by a small group of intrepid pioneers and now carry millions of passengers each year, "space planes" may one day be an equally popular transportation.

When orbiting around the Earth, the **Hubble Space Telescope** is able to give astronomers sharper photographs of the stars and galaxies than is possible from the Earth's surface. This is because the Earth's atmosphere distorts images of space.

Salyut I space station

119

What is a spacecraft?

Spacecraft are vehicles designed to travel in space. They include satellites orbiting the Earth, probes sent to the planets, and manned vehicles such as the American *Space Shuttle* and Russian *Soyuz* craft. They are launched by immensely powerful rockets. In space, they steer by firing smaller thrusters.

Robert H. Goddard, an American scientist, launched the first liquid-fuel rocket at Auburn, Massachusetts, on March 16, 1926. It flew 184 ft. (56 m) in 2.5 seconds.

The German **V-2** was the first successful modern rocket. It stood 56 ft. (14 m) high and weighed 27,500 lb (12,500 kg).

Warhead

Alcohol fuel tank

Liquid oxygen tank

V-2 rocket

German scientists and engineers developed the V-2 rocket weapon during World War II (1939–45). It carried a 2,200 lb (1,000 kg) warhead a distance of 171 mi. (275 km), flying faster than the speed of sound.

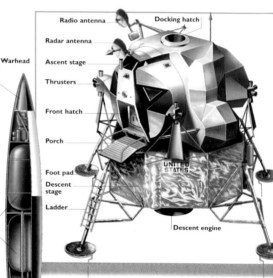

Radio antenna

Docking hatch

Radar antenna

Ascent stage

Thrusters

Front hatch

Porch

Foot pad

Descent stage

Ladder

UNITED STATES

Descent engine

Spacecraft

All spacecraft need electricity to power their instruments and communication equipment. Most spacecraft make electricity from sunlight by using solar panels. Beyond the orbit of Mars, there is too little sunlight for solar panels to work, so space probes going to the outer planets use nuclear generators. American manned spacecraft use fuel cells to make electricity from a chemical reaction between hydrogen and oxygen.

ERS-1

Remote sensing

Remote sensing satellites collect information about the Earth or another planet from space. The European remote sensing satellite (*ERS-1*) was launched in 1991 to study the Earth, its oceans, and atmosphere.

Rocket types

Rockets like the European *Ariane* launcher, burn liquid fuel. *Ariane*'s liquid engines are assisted by two strap-on solid propellant engines. Burning requires oxygen, so the fuel is mixed with a liquid called an oxidizer that provides the oxygen. Liquid fuel rocket engines are controllable. They can be turned on and off, and varied in power, by pumping more or less fuel into the engine. Another type of rocket burns solid propellant, a mixture of solid fuel and oxidizer. Once lit, it burns until no propellant is left.

Spacecraft anatomy

The *Apollo Lunar Excursion Module* (*LEM*) could land two astronauts on the Moon. It was a very unusual spacecraft. The base, or descent stage, had a rocket engine to slow down the *LEM* for landing. Then, at the end of the mission, the *LEM* split in two, and the descent stage formed a launch pad for the upper part, or ascent stage. It steered by firing thrusters arranged in groups of four. Broad foot pads kept it from sinking into the Moon's surface.

- Payload
- 3rd stage
- 2nd stage
- Propellant
- Oxidizer
- 1st stage
- Booster rocket

ARIANE

SOLID ROCKET BOOSTER

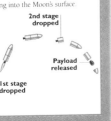

- **2nd stage dropped**
- **Payload released**
- **1st stage dropped**
- **Booster dropped**
- **Lift off**

Rocket launch

A rocket is actually several rockets, called stages, stacked on top of each other. Each stage falls away as it runs out of fuel.

- Nuclear power generator
- Radio dish

GALILEO

Space probes

Unmanned space probes have visited and studied most of the planets and many of their moons. The *Galileo* probe, launched in 1989, studied Jupiter and its moons in the 1990s.

121

Satellites and probes

The Space Age began on October 4, 1957, when Russia sent the first man-made object into orbit. It was called *Sputnik*, (meaning "traveler"). Other unmanned spacecraft were launched to explore the solar system. They landed on the Moon, photographed the planets, mapped Venus, and looked for life on Mars. Today, satellites orbit the Earth to monitor the weather, and others study the universe with telescopes. Probes have visited Jupiter and the outer planets, acting as the robot eyes and ears of scientists and astronauts who may follow them one day.

Sputnik-1

A metal ball with a radio transmitter, *Sputnik-1* had four long aerials to send its bleeps to an amazed world. Its launch sparked a "space race" between the U.S. and Russia that lasted until *Apollo 11* in 1969.

Sputnik-1

Country: Russia
Date: 1957
Size: 2 ft. (58 cm) across
Construction: metal sphere
Top speed: 17,500 mph (28,000 km/h)

Surveyor 3

Landing on a part of the Moon called the Ocean of Storms, *Surveyor 3* took 6,315 photographs of the Moon's surface. It dug a small trench in the ground to test the Moon's strength in preparation for later manned landings. In 1969, *Apollo 12* landed near the craft and astronauts brought parts of the *Surveyor* back to Earth.

Surveyor 3

Country: U.S.A.
Date: 1967
Size: 10 ft. (3 m) high
Construction: lightweight alloys
Top speed: 24,230 mph (39,000 km/h)

Viking

In 1976, two *Viking* spacecraft went into orbit around the planet Mars. They dropped probes onto the surface. The landers carried a chemical laboratory, a weather station that sent daily reports until 1983, and an instrument to study Mars-quakes. They took thousands of photographs, and also tested samples of the rust-red soil for signs of life on Mars. No life forms were detected.

Viking

Country: U.S.A.
Date: 1976
Size: 9¼ ft. (3 m)
Construction: lightweight alloys
Top speed: 24,230 mph (39,000 km/h)

Voyager

The first close-up images and measurements of distant planets were taken by Voyager. New moons and rings around Jupiter were revealed. The instruments ran on nuclear power, and a radio dish 12 ft. (3.7 m) across kept the probe in contact with Earth.

Voyager

Country: U.S.A.
Date: 1977
Size: 9¾ ft. (3 m) high
Construction: aluminum
Top speed: 32,000 mph (52,000 km/h)

Country: U.S.A.
Date: 1990
Size: 43¼ ft. (13.3 m) long
Construction: lightweight alloys
Top speed: 17,500 mph (28,000 km/h)

Galileo

In 1995, Galileo became the first spacecraft to orbit Jupiter. It was named after the great Italian scientist, Galileo Galilei, who discovered four of Jupiter's moons. A small probe was dropped into Jupiter's atmosphere. This sent back measurements for 57 minutes until it was destroyed by heat and crushing pressure.

Galileo

Hubble Space Telescope

This orbiting telescope has given astronomers amazing pictures of stars forming and exploding with no interference from the Earth's atmosphere. But the first images were blurred because a mistake had been made when making the telescope's main mirror. Space Shuttle astronauts repaired the telescope using the Canadarm.

Hubble Space Telescope

Country: U.S.A.
Date: 1989
Size: 17½ ft. (5.3 m) high
Construction: lightweight alloys
Top speed: 54,225 mph (86,760 km/h)

Cassini-Huygens

The largest space probe ever launched, Cassini-Huygens is two space probes in one. The main craft, Cassini, will study the ringed planet Saturn in 2004. It carries Huygens, a smaller probe which it will drop on to Saturn's largest moon, Titan. If Huygens survives the landing, it will test whether the surface is solid or liquid.

Cassini-Huygens

Country: U.S.A., Europe
Date: 1997
Size: 22¼ ft. (6.8 m) high
Construction: lightweight alloys
Top speed: 42,511 mph (68,400 km/h)

123

Taking Man to the Moon

A new age in exploration and transportation began when Russian cosmonaut Yuri Gagarin became the first person to be launched into space. He made one orbit in his tiny capsule and returned safely to Earth. Not to be outdone, the United States launched its own series of manned spaceflights to learn how to control spacecraft and link them together. The "space race" was on and was "won" by the *Apollo* spacecraft landing 12 astronauts on the Moon between 1969 and 1972.

Vostok 1

Mercury Redstone 3

Country: Russia
Date: 1961
Size: 7½ ft. (2.3 m)
Construction: lightweight alloys
Top speed: 17,500 mph (28,000 km/h)
On board: 1

Mercury Redstone 3

The first American astronaut in space was Alan Shepard on board *Mercury Redstone 3* (MR-3). A *Redstone* rocket boosted his capsule *Freedom 7* to a height of 116½ mi. (187.5 km). There was not enough power to place the capsule in orbit, so it re-entered the atmosphere and fell back to Earth.

Country: U.S.A.
Date: 1961
Size: 9½ ft. (2.9 m)
Construction: lightweight alloys
Top speed: 5,180 mph (8,336 km/h)
On board: 1

Vostok 1

The *Vostok 1* (meaning "east" in Russian) space capsule was a hollow metal ball just big enough for Yuri Gagarin to lie down inside for the flight lasting 1 hour 48 minutes. It was completely covered with heat-shield material to protect him from the intense heat of re-entering the atmosphere. A rocket engine on the capsule was fired after one orbit to slow the capsule and make it fall back to Earth.

Mercury Atlas MA-6

John Glenn was the first American astronaut to orbit the Earth. His Mercury capsule, *Friendship 7*, was launched by an *Atlas* rocket (more powerful than the *Redstone* rockets on the early *Mercury* flights). After three orbits when it seemed that the capsule's heat shield had come loose, Glenn's flight was cut short for fear it would burn up on re-entering the atmosphere. But Glenn landed safely.

Mercury Atlas MA-6

Country: U.S.A.
Date: 1962
Size: 9½ ft. (2.9 m)
Construction: lightweight alloys
Top speed: 17,543 mph (28,234 km/h)
On board: 1

Gemini 6

Twice the size and weight of *Mercury*, the *Gemini* spacecraft carried a two-man crew. There were 10 *Gemini* flights in less than two years. *Gemini 6* was to be launched to maneuver close to a rocket already in space. But the rocket was lost, and *Gemini 6* was delayed a few months so it could use *Gemini 7* as its target instead. *Gemini 6*, flown by Wally Schirra and Thomas Stafford, came within 12 in. (0.3 m) of *Gemini 7*.

Country: U.S.A.
Date: 1965
Size: 18½ ft. (5.6 m)
Body: lightweight alloys
Top speed: 17,500 mph (28,000 km/h)
On board: 2

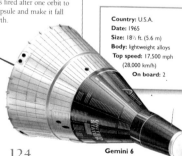
Gemini 6

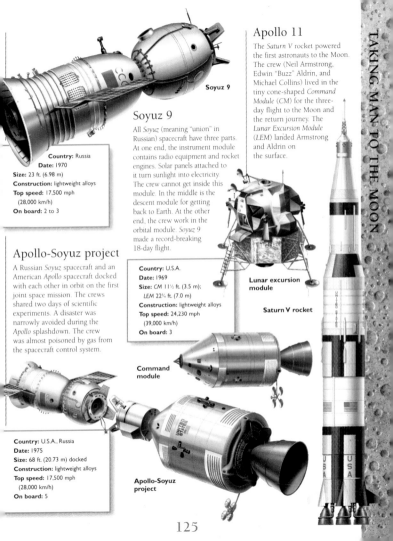

Apollo 11

The *Saturn V* rocket powered the first astronauts to the Moon. The crew (Neil Armstrong, Edwin "Buzz" Aldrin, and Michael Collins) lived in the tiny cone-shaped *Command Module* (CM) for the three-day flight to the Moon and the return journey. The *Lunar Excursion Module* (LEM) landed Armstrong and Aldrin on the surface.

Soyuz 9

All *Soyuz* (meaning "union" in Russian) spacecraft have three parts. At one end, the instrument module contains radio equipment and rocket engines. Solar panels attached to it turn sunlight into electricity The crew cannot get inside this module. In the middle is the descent module for getting back to Earth. At the other end, the crew work in the orbital module. *Soyuz 9* made a record-breaking 18-day flight.

Soyuz 9

Country: Russia
Date: 1970
Size: 23 ft. (6.98 m)
Construction: lightweight alloys
Top speed: 17,500 mph (28,000 km/h)
On board: 2 to 3

Country: U.S.A.
Date: 1969
Size: CM 11½ ft. (3.5 m); LEM 22¼ ft. (7.0 m)
Construction: lightweight alloys
Top speed: 24,230 mph (39,000 km/h)
On board: 3

Lunar excursion module

Saturn V rocket

Apollo-Soyuz project

A Russian *Soyuz* spacecraft and an American *Apollo* spacecraft docked with each other in orbit on the first joint space mission. The crews shared two days of scientific experiments. A disaster was narrowly avoided during the *Apollo* splashdown. The crew was almost poisoned by gas from the spacecraft control system.

Command module

Country: U.S.A., Russia
Date: 1975
Size: 68 ft. (20.73 m) docked
Construction: lightweight alloys
Top speed: 17,500 mph (28,000 km/h)
On board: 5

Apollo-Soyuz project

The Space Shuttle

The space shuttle is the first reusable spacecraft. It blasts off like a rocket and lands again like an airliner on a runway. Within 14 days it can be ready for another flight. Its main job is to carry satellites, experiments, and parts of the planned international space station into orbit. The immense thrust needed to launch the winged craft, which is called the orbiter, is supplied by three main engines in its tail, fed with fuel from an external tank and two solid rocket boosters.

A **space shuttle** launch is a spectacular sight. As space shuttle *Endeavour* takes off (*above*), searing hot gases race out of the orbiter's engines and its rocket boosters at 620 mph (10,000 km/h).

The orbiter

The orbiter is the space-plane of the space shuttle: it is 120 ft. (37 m) long with a wingspan of 79 ft. (24 m)—about the same size as a small plane like the Boeing 737. It can carry a crew of up to seven into Earth orbit.

The launch

The shuttle blasts off using the orbiter's main engines and two solid rocket boosters (**1**). Two minutes later, at a height of 28 mi. (45 km), the boosters fall away (**2**). They land in the Atlantic Ocean by parachute. Ships pick them up so they can be refueled for another flight. At a height of 70 mi. (113 km), 8.5 minutes into the flight, the almost empty external tank (**3**) falls into the Indian Ocean.

Remote manipulator arm

Flight deck

Thrusters

Liquid oxygen tank

Liquid hydrogen tank

3.

2.

1.

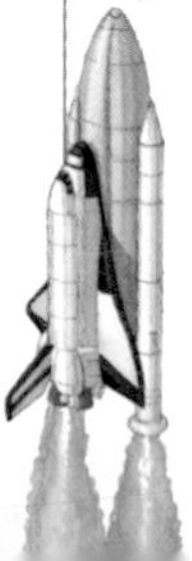

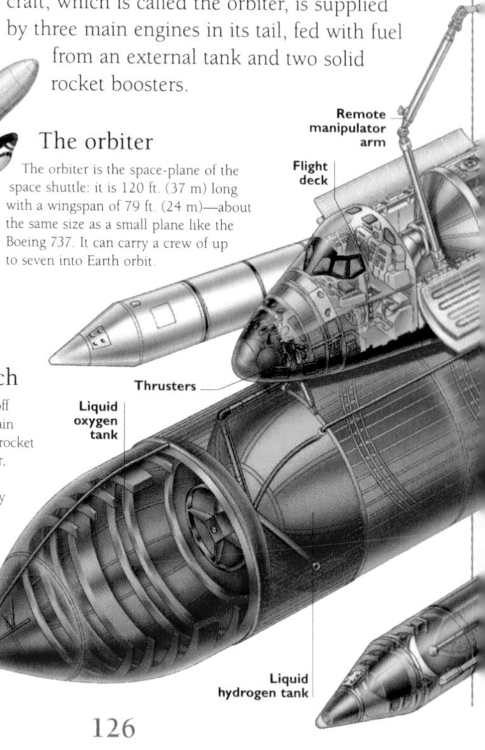

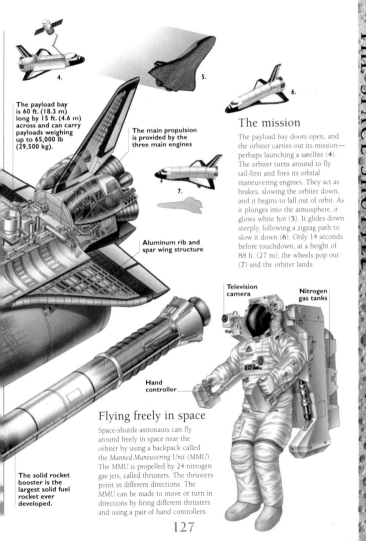

4.

5.

6.

The payload bay is 60 ft. (18.3 m) long by 15 ft. (4.6 m) across and can carry payloads weighing up to 65,000 lb (29,500 kg).

The main propulsion is provided by the three main engines

7.

Aluminum rib and spar wing structure

The mission

The payload bay doors open, and the orbiter carries out its mission—perhaps launching a satellite (**4**). The orbiter turns around to fly tail-first and fires its orbital maneuvering engines. They act as brakes, slowing the orbiter down, and it begins to fall out of orbit. As it plunges into the atmosphere, it glows white hot (**5**). It glides down steeply, following a zigzag path to slow it down (**6**). Only 14 seconds before touchdown, at a height of 88 ft. (27 m), the wheels pop out (**7**) and the orbiter lands.

Television camera

Nitrogen gas tanks

Hand controller

The solid rocket booster is the largest solid fuel rocket ever developed.

Flying freely in space

Space-shuttle astronauts can fly around freely in space near the orbiter by using a backpack called the *Manned Maneuvering Unit (MMU)*. The *MMU* is propelled by 24 nitrogen gas jets, called thrusters. The thrusters point in different directions. The *MMU* can be made to move or turn in directions by firing different thrusters and using a pair of hand controllers.

127

Space Stations

A space station is a large craft that stays in space for several months or years, and is visited by different crews. Docking ports allow spacecraft to dock (connect) with the station. Early space stations were launched complete, but larger modern space stations are now launched in pieces and assembled in space. These craft let scientists carry out long-term experiments and observations, for example, to study the effects of long space missions on the human body, which will be very important should we one day send people to the planets.

Salyut 1

The first space station, *Salyut* (Russian for "salute") *1*, was launched on April 19, 1971, into an orbit 124 mi. (200 km) above the Earth. Two *Soyuz* crews (see page 125) visited the station before it re-entered the atmosphere on October 11, 1971, and burned up. *Salyut 1* carried two telescopes for observing the stars. The cosmonauts carried out medical experiments on each other and studied how plants grow in space.

Salyut 1

> **Country:** Russia
> **Date:** 1971
> **Size:** 42¾ ft. (13 m)
> **Construction:** aluminum, steel
> **Top speed:** 17,500 mph
> (28,000 km/h)
> **On board:** Up to 5 crew

Skylab

Skylab was the first American space station. It was made from an empty fuel tank from a *Saturn* rocket (see page 125). Severe vibration during launch tore off a shield and solar panel, but *Skylab* survived. Three crews, each with three astronauts, spent 171 days inside it. They took 182,000 photographs of the Sun, 40,000 of the Earth, and 2,500 of Comet *Kahoutek*. They also carried out many scientific experiments. The abandoned *Skylab* crashed to Earth in July 1979.

Skylab

> **Country:** U.S.A.
> **Date:** 1973
> **Size:** 84 ft. (25.6 m)
> **Construction:** aluminum, steel
> **Top speed:** 17,500 mph
> (28,000 km/h)
> **On board:** 3 crew

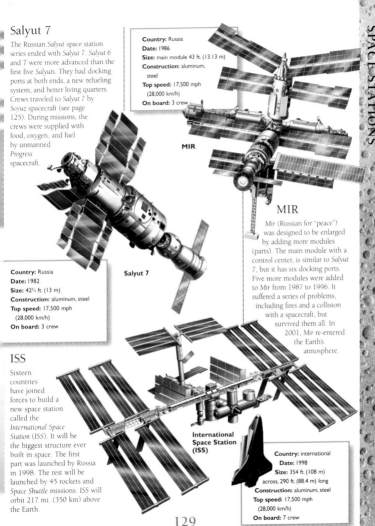

Salyut 7

The Russian *Salyut* space station series ended with *Salyut 7*. *Salyut 6* and 7 were more advanced than the first five *Salyuts*. They had docking ports at both ends, a new refueling system, and better living quarters. Crews traveled to *Salyut 7* by *Soyuz* spacecraft (see page 125). During missions, the crews were supplied with food, oxygen, and fuel by unmanned *Progress* spacecraft.

Country: Russia
Date: 1986
Size: main module 43 ft. (13.13 m)
Construction: aluminum, steel
Top speed: 17,500 mph (28,000 km/h)
On board: 3 crew

MIR

Salyut 7

Country: Russia
Date: 1982
Size: 42¼ ft. (13 m)
Construction: aluminum, steel
Top speed: 17,500 mph (28,000 km/h)
On board: 3 crew

MIR

Mir (Russian for "peace") was designed to be enlarged by adding more modules (parts). The main module with a control center, is similar to *Salyut 7*, but it has six docking ports. Five more modules were added to *Mir* from 1987 to 1996. It suffered a series of problems, including fires and a collision with a spacecraft, but survived them all. In 2001, *Mir* re-entered the Earth's atmosphere.

ISS

Sixteen countries have joined forces to build a new space station called the *International Space Station* (ISS). It will be the biggest structure ever built in space. The first part was launched by Russia in 1998. The rest will be launched by 45 rockets and *Space Shuttle* missions. *ISS* will orbit 217 mi. (350 km) above the Earth.

International Space Station (ISS)

Country: international
Date: 1998
Size: 354 ft. (108 m) across, 290 ft. (88.4 m) long
Construction: aluminum, steel
Top speed: 17,500 mph (28,000 km/h)
On board: 7 crew

Into the Unknown

Transportation in the most remote places and in extreme conditions calls for extraordinary vehicles. Deep-sea explorers travel inside a thick metal sphere that protects them from the crushing water pressure. Scientists who work in the icy polar regions use tracked vehicles to travel across snow. The tracks spread the vehicle's weight and help to stop it from sinking into the snow. The remotest places of all, other worlds, are explored by robot vehicles. They have driven across the Moon and Mars, guided by drivers on Earth linked to the vehicles by radio.

Mathematician David Bushnell's **Turtle** (1776) was a forerunner of the modern submarine. It only carried one man, who had to crank the propeller by hand, adjust the water ballast (weight), and steer with very tiny portholes to peer through.

On January 23, 1960, **Jacques Piccard** and **Don Walsh** climbed into their bathyscaphe, **Trieste**, and sank 35,805 ft. (10,916 m) to the bottom of the Mariana Trench in the Pacific Ocean. It is still the deepest manned dive ever made.

In 1997, the **Sojourner rover** (*left*) spent 85 days exploring the surface of Mars, studying rocks until its power source failed.

The crews of **Apollo 15, 16,** and **17** took an electric car, the **Apollo lunar rover** (*right*), to the Moon to travel farther across the surface than earlier astronauts.

Using a car instead of dogs or horses to pull sleds on his 1907–09 Antarctic expedition was not a success for **Ernest Shackleton.**

The Soviet Union landed two unmanned electric vehicles, **Lunokhod 1** and **2,** on the Moon in the 1970s (*below*). The 1,667 lb (756 kg) vehicles sent 100,000 photographs of the Moon to Earth. They also analyzed the strength and chemistry of the Moon's surface.

Timeline of Transportation

Thousands of years ago, Pacific island fishing boats use outriggers (balancing floats) to keep upright against the currents and winds.

Italian inventor Leonardo da Vinci (1452–1519) sketches the first helicopter and parachute. In 2000 his wooden and canvas parachute is recreated and flies from 20,000 ft. (6,000 m).

George and Robert Stephenson's Rocket is the first express passenger locomotive, reaching a speed of 29 mph (47 km/h).

Karl Benz drives his motorized tricycle in 1885 at the speed of a trotting horse.

1852 Frenchman Henri Giffard flies the first steam airship

1859 Ironclads, warships whose wooden hulls are protected by iron plates, are introduced. The first is the French vessel, *La Gloire*.

1859 Frenchman Etienne Lenoir builds the first internal combustion engine. It is powered by gas.

1863 The first underground rail system, with steam locomotives, opens in London.

1869 The Central Pacific and Union Pacific railroads meet to form the country's first coast-to-coast railroad.

1879 The first electric railroad is built in Berlin, Germany.

1883 The *Orient Express* train service begins to carry passengers between Paris and Constantinople (modern Istanbul), Turkey.

1885 Karl Benz, a German engineer, builds the world's first gasoline-driven car.

1885 The British *Rover* safety bicycle is the first with equal-sized wheels and a chain drive.

1892 German engineer Rudolf Diesel patents a new form of engine that will be named after him.

1897 *Turbinia*, a small turbine-driven steam vessel, breaks speed records. Soon many ships will be powered by turbines.

1903 The Wright brothers make the first powered flights in their airplane, *The Flyer*, at Kitty Hawk, North Carolina.

1908 The *Model T Ford*, the most successful of the early mass-produced cars, begins production in the Detroit, Michigan.

The first modern-looking bicycles, such as the *Rover*, with chains, spokes, and equal-sized inflatable tires appear in 1885.

The first single-rotor helicopter is developed by Igor Sikorsky in 1939.

1910 The first seaplane is built by French engineer Henri Fabre.

1912 The world's largest liner, *Titanic*, sinks on her maiden voyage when it hits an iceberg.

1914 The Atlantic and Pacific oceans are linked with the opening of the Panama Canal.

1919 British flyers John Alcock and Arthur Whitten-Brown make the first nonstop flight across the Atlantic.

1920 The first aircraft with a retracting undercarriage, the *Dayton-Wright RB* monoplane, is produced.

1923 Aircraft carriers are built for the British and Japanese navies.

1929 Synchromesh, a new design feature on a transmission, is introduced by the General Motors Corporation. It makes changing gears much easier.

1933 With the 247, the Boeing Corporation introduces the first modern airliner.

1936 The Volkswagen *Beetle*, the first "people's car," is designed.

1937 British inventor Frank Whittle builds the world's first jet engine.

1939 The first practical helicopter is designed by Igor Sikorsky.

1947 The American Bell X-1 rocket plane becomes the first vehicle to break the sound barrier.

1952 The De Havilland Company introduces the *Comet*, the first jet airliner.

1955 The first nuclear-powered submarine, the American *Nautilus*, enters service.

1957 Russia launches *Sputnik I*, the first artificial satellite to orbit the Earth.

The Volkswagen *Beetle* ("People's wagon") is designed by Dr. Ferdinand Porsche in 1936. Since then more than 20 million of these cars have been sold in 30 countries.

Sputnik I is launched in 1957, and the "space race" begins.

1959 The Austin Mini goes on the market.

1959 The first practical hovercraft is demonstrated.

1961 The Soviet spacecraft *Vostok I* carries cosmonaut Yuri Gagarin, the first human to travel into space.

1964 Super-fast "bullet trains" begin to transform travel in Japan.

1969 The American spacecraft *Apollo 11* takes the first astronauts to the Moon.

1969 *Concorde*, the supersonic airliner makes its first test flight.

1969 The Boeing 747, or jumbo jet, flies for the first time.

1970 *Salyut 1*, the first space station, is orbiting the Earth.

1976 Two unmanned *Viking* spacecraft land on the planet Mars.

1981 The space shuttle *Columbia* makes its first flight.

1981 The French high-speed train, the *TGV*, starts to carry passengers.

1989 The American stealth bomber, the *Northrop B-2*, flies for the first time.

1990 General Motors develops a battery-powered car that could point the way to the future of road transportation.

1994 The Channel Tunnel opens, linking Britain and France by rail.

2001 Space station *Mir* re-enters Earth's atmosphere after 15 years in orbit.

The Japanese *Shinkansen*, or *Bullet Train*, has a maximum service speed of 137 mph (220 km/h).

Transportation Trailblazers

Armstrong, Neil, American astronaut
(1930–) Born in Ohio, Armstrong was a pilot
and test pilot before being selected as an astronaut
in 1962. On July 20, 1969, he was the first person
to land on the Moon, speaking the famous words,
"That's one small step for [a] man, one giant leap
for mankind."

Beebe, Charles, American naturalist and
explorer (1877–1962) Beebe was an expert
on birds who was also interested in exploring
under the sea. Together with engineer Otis
Barton, he created the bathysphere, a spherical
diving vessel which they took to the record
depth of 3,028 ft. (923 m).

Benz, Karl, German engineer (1844–1929)
Benz built the world's first gasoline-driven motor
car, which took to being road in 1885.

Blériot, Louis, French aviator (1872–1936)
Blériot made the first flight across the
English Channel on July 25, 1909. He flew
a 24-horsepower monoplane that he had
built himself.

Braun, Wernher von, German-American
rocket scientist (1912–77) Born in Germany,
Wernher von Braun developed the V-2 rocket
weapons used during World War II. After the war
he moved to the U.S., where he worked on the
rockets for the first Earth satellites and on the
Saturn rockets used for the Apollo moon landing.

Campbell, Donald, British racing driver
(1921–67) Campbell set several speed records,
both on land and on the water, following
his father's land-speed record of 174 mph
(280 km/h) in 1927. Donald died on Coniston
Water in England during his attempt to be the
first person to travel at over 483 mph (300 mph)
on water. His own son Donald Wales broke the
British land speed record for electric vehicles
in 2000 with a speed of 128 mph (205 km/h).

Cayley, George, British scientist
(1773–1857) One of the earliest pioneers of
aeronautics, Cayley created the first practical
glider to carry a person. He realized that
powered flight would have to wait until
a light but powerful engine could be built.

Cierva, Juan de la, Spanish engineer
(1895–1936) Fascinated by flying from an early
age, Cierva used his engineering skills to invent and
build the autogiro, a forerunner of the helicopter
that has both a rotor and an airplane propeller.

Cockerell, Christopher, British inventor
(1910–2000) Cockerell worked on radar in
World War II, but is famous for inventing the
hovercraft, a vehicle that rides on a cushion
of air. Cockerell had made a working model
hovercraft by 1955. Four years later, a hovercraft
was crossing the English Channel.

Cook, James, British explorer (1728–79)
One of the greatest navigators of all time,
Cook traveled to the Pacific, sailing along
the coasts of Australia, New Zealand, and many
Pacific islands. He also discovered how to keep
people healthy on long voyages. By feeding fresh
fruit to his crew, he kept them clear of scurvy,
a disease that had plagued sailors for centuries.

Cugnot, Nicholas, French military engineer
(1725–1804) Responding to the needs of the
army, Cugnot invented a three-wheeled gun
carriage that was the first practical steam-driven
vehicle. Its top speed was only 3 mph (3.2 km/h),
so it did not catch on, and Cugnot had no money
to build an improved version.

Daimler, Gottlieb, German inventor
(1834–1900) Daimler built a number of
improved gas engines before starting work
on powered vehicles. In the 1880s he built
very cars and motorcycles.

De Havilland, Geoffrey, British aircraft
designer (1882–1965) After building his
first aircraft himself in 1908, De Havilland
ran a company that came up with some of
the most successful aircraft of the time. Its
48-seater jet airliner, the Comet, was the first
of its type, and helped bring about long-distance
mass air travel.

Diesel, Rudolf, German engineer
(1858–1913) During the 1880s, Rudolf Diesel
began work to produce a more efficient internal-
combustion engine. He came up with a design in
which the fuel ignites at high pressure and which
is still widely used in trucks, buses, and cars. This
type of engine is known as the diesel engine.

Dunlop, John Boyd, Scottish inventor
(1840–1921) A Scottish vet working in Belfast,
Northern Ireland, Dunlop fitted his son's tricycle
with air-filled rubber tires in 1887. In doing this,
he was reinventing an earlier idea. Dunlop went
on to make money from his tires, founding the
Dunlop Rubber Company to make air-filled tires.

Farman, Henri, French aviator (1874–1958)
Farman was one of the first men to fly, piloting
the first Voisin biplane in 1908. He then went into
business to build biplanes, and in 1917 made the
Goliath bomber, which was converted in 1919 to
one of the first airliners.

Ford, Henry, American car manufacturer
(1863–1947) Beginning by making cars himself,
Ford founded the Ford Motor Company in 1903.
Five years later, he was producing the Model T,
the first successful mass-produced car. In all, 15
million Model Ts were made, bringing driving
within the reach of ordinary Americans.

Fulton, Robert, American inventor
(1765–1815) Trained as a painter, Fulton
became an engineer during the 1790s. His
many inventions included a machine for cutting
and polishing marble and a submarine torpedo
boat. He is most famous as a pioneer of the
steamboat. His vessel Clermont, launched on
New York's Hudson River in 1806, was the first
successful steamer.

Gagarin, Yuri, Russian (Soviet) cosmonaut
(1934–68) Gagarin was the first man in space.
He orbited the Earth in his spaceship, Vostok,
in 1961, returning to Earth a Russian hero.

Goddard, Robert, American physicist
(1882–1945) One of the greatest pioneers of
rocketry, Goddard was little known in his lifetime.
He developed the liquid-fuel rocket, built rockets
capable of greater and greater speeds, and invented
methods of controlling them as they flew. Only after
his death was his work recognized.

Goodyear, Charles, American inventor
(1800–60) Charles Goodyear spent some 10
years of his life researching and experimenting
with rubber. His most important achievement
was the invention of vulcanizing (toughening
rubber by curing it with sulfur), without which
road vehicle tires would not have been practical.

Harrison, John, British clockmaker
(1693–1776) In 1713 the British government
offered a prize for the person who came up with
an accurate method of calculating longitude at
sea. To do this, you need to be able to tell the
time, and Harrison set himself the difficult task of
making a clock that would be accurate on board
ship. He created a series of highly accurate clocks
that finally enabled sailors to figure out exactly
where they were, and, after years of effort, was
awarded the prize.

134

Henry the Navigator, Prince of Portugal (1394–1460) Prince Henry founded a navigation school, set up an observatory, and sent ships across the seas on voyages of exploration. His work paved the way for a great age of sea voyages, during which explorers from Europe were some of the first to visit Africa and America.

Issigonis, Alec, British car designer (1906–88) Born in Turkey, Issigonis moved to Britain in his teens. His most famous design was the *Mini*, which appeared in 1959 and transformed small cars all over the world.

Johnson, Amy, British aviator (1903–41) Amy Johnson was one of the first women to learn to fly. She made many long-distance flights, most famously from England to Australia in 1930.

Jouffroy d'Abbas, Claude, French inventor (1751–1832) The French nobleman Claude Jouffroy d'Abbas built the first really practical steamboat in 1783. However, his work was ignored until steamboats were taken up by inventors like Robert Fulton.

Lenoir, Étienne, French engineer (1822–1900) The internal combustion engine was invented by French engineer Étienne Lenoir. Lenoir's original engine was fueled by coal gas, but later versions were used in gasoline-powered cars and airplanes.

Lilienthal, Otto, German inventor (1849–96) Lilienthal was a great pioneer of the glider and made many flights in craft that he built himself. He studied the flight of birds, hoping to build a flying machine with flapping wings. Lilienthal fell to his death during one of his flights.

McAdam, John, Scottish engineer (1756–1836) McAdam had a career in business in the U.S. before settling back in Scotland to invent a better way of building roads. He developed a hard-wearing road surface using gravel and crushed stone, and raised them so they drained properly. The word "tarmac" is derived from this inventor's name.

Messerschmidt, Willy, German aircraft manufacturer (1898–1978) During the mid-20th century, Messerschmidt's company produced aircraft such as the *Me.109*, the fastest airplane in the world in 1939, and the *Me.262*, the first jet aircraft to fly in World War II.

Montgolfier brothers, French balloonists Joseph Michel (1740–1810) and Jacques Étienne Montgolfier (1745–99) These brothers constructed the first hot-air balloon in 1782. In 1783 they launched the first manned balloon flight, taking two of their friends some 3,000 ft. (915 m) high.

Olds, Ransom, American car manufacturer (1864–1950) After trying steam-powered cars, Ransom Olds began to make gasoline-driven Oldsmobiles in 1899. Later he pioneered the assembly-line method of production, which was taken up even more successfully by Henry Ford.

Otto, Nikolaus, German engineer (1832–91) Otto was a pioneer of the internal combustion engine. He invented the four-stroke cycle, the principle still used in car engines today.

Parsons, Charles, Irish engineer (1854–1931) After training as an engineer, Parsons developed the high-speed steam turbine, a device that transformed ship propulsion and electricity generation. He first became famous when his turbine-driven steamship, the *Turbinia*, broke all speed records.

Plimsoll, Samuel, British politician (1824–98) A member of the British Parliament, Samuel Plimsoll was concerned about the safety of overloaded merchant ships that sat too low in the water. He introduced a mark, which was painted on the hull of every merchant ship, showing the point down to which the ship could be loaded. This mark is still called the Plimsoll line.

Porsche, Ferdinand, German car designer (1875–1951) Porsche began as a designer for German companies such as Daimler before he went on to design the famous Volkswagen *Beetle*, and later the *Porsche* sports car.

Pullman, George, American businessman (1831–97) The luxurious Pullman sleeping car was patented in 1864 and 1865, after which George Pullman founded a company to produce and sell his invention. Pullman also invented the railroad dining car and devised a way of connecting railroad cars with covered passages.

Royce, Henry, British engineer (1863–1933) Royce was an electrical engineer who became interested in cars. He made his first car in 1904, and his work so impressed Charles Rolls (1877–1910) that they joined to form Rolls-Royce, making luxury cars and aircraft engines.

Sikorsky, Igor, Russian-American engineer (1889–1972) As a young man, Sikorsky wanted to produce a craft that could take off vertically, so he came up with the idea of the helicopter, with its spinning rotor. He made his first successful helicopter in 1939, and all later helicopters have been based on this design.

Stephenson, British engineers, George (1781–1848) and his son Robert (1803–59) George and Robert were important railroad pioneers. They worked together on the Stockton and Darlington and Liverpool and Manchester railways, and on the famous locomotive, the *Rocket*, which set new standards for both speed and reliability.

Tereshkova, Valentina, Russian (Soviet) cosmonaut (1937–) The first woman to fly in space, Valentina Tereshkova, piloted the spacecraft *Vostok 6* in 1963. She completed 48 Earth orbits in her three-day flight.

Trevithick, Richard, British engineer (1771–1833) Richard Trevithick worked as a mining engineer and made several steam road vehicles before building the first steam railroad locomotives.

Westinghouse, George, American inventor (1846–1914) Among Westinghouse's many inventions in the field of engineering, the most famous was the air brake. This allowed a train driver to control the brakes on all the train's cars at once. This made trains safer and able to go at higher speeds.

Whittle, Frank, British engineer (1907–96) As a student, Whittle began the research that led to the jet engine. His work was ignored by the authorities, but he carried on, patenting his first jet engine in 1930. By 1941, a British jet-powered aircraft, a *Gloster E28/39*, was in the air.

Wright, American pioneers of flying, Orville (1871–1948) and Wilbur (1867–1912) The Wright brothers made the first powered flight ever, in their own-designed glider.

Zeppelin, Count Ferdinand von, German airship manufacturer (1838–1917) Zeppelin was an army officer who became interested in flight. He made his first airship in 1900. Soon, whenever people thought of airships, they thought of Zeppelin.

Transportation Record Breakers

On wheels

First car
The first gasoline-engine car was built by Karl Benz of Mannheim, Germany, in 1885 (see page 16). It was a three-wheeler and could travel at about 8 mph (13 km/h).

Most popular cars
The first really popular car was the *Model T Ford* (see page 20), which was made from 1908 to 1927. At that time, around 15 million *Model Ts* were made. They are still being driven today by car enthusiasts. But more Volkswagen *Beetles* (see page 20) were produced than any other type of car. When production in Germany stopped in the early 1970s, there were over 16 million *Beetles*.

Most economical vehicle
Probably the best fuel consumption figures to date were achieved by a vehicle designed by *Honda* during a contest in Finland in 1996. The *Honda* managed 9,426 mpg (3,336 km/litre)—250 times better than many standard family cars.

Fastest car
The world's fastest car is *Thrust SSC* (see page 42), which is powered by two jet engines. *Thrust SSC*, driven by Andy Green of Britain, was the first car to go faster than the speed of sound.

Fastest racing car
The racing cars that travel fastest are drag racers (see page 42), which move from standing to speeds of over 310 mph (500 km/h) on a course of just 1,320 ft. (402 m). The world record was set by American driver Gary Scelzi, who reached 326½ mph (522.3 km/h) in 1998.

Fastest production car
The *McLaren F1* is the fastest car that can be driven on the road. It is capable of speeds of up to 240 mph (386.7 km/h) and can accelerate from 0–60 mph (0 to 96 km/h) in a little over three seconds.

Longest car
People often try to build cars that are long enough to beat the world record. These machines are so long that they are not practical

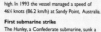

Peterbilt truck

road-going vehicles—but they make interesting displays at fairs and exhibitions. Probably the longest to date measures 100 ft. (30.5 m) and was designed by Jay Ohrberg. The American vehicle has 24 wheels, and there is a small swimming pool, complete with a diving board, in the rear.

Ferrari 250 GTO

Longest bicycle
The longest modern bicycle was made during the 1980s, measuring 73 ft. (22.2 m) long, and was ridden by four people. But in the late 19th century, a 10-person bicycle, called *La Décuplette*, was built in France.

Fastest cyclist
Some cyclists have traveled faster than most people have ever managed in a car. This is because a cycle can pick up speed when traveling in the slipstream of a powered vehicle. The fastest to date was the Dutch cyclist Fred Rompelberg, who clocked up an amazing 167 mph (268.8 km/h) in 1995.

On water

First round-the-world
Portuguese navigator Ferdinand Magellan embarked with five ships to sail all around the world in 1519. During the journey Magellan and most of his crew of 260 men died, but in 1522 one of his ships with 18 aboard completed the voyage.

First across the Atlantic
The first likely sailors to have crossed the Atlantic were Viking seamen in around 1001. This was the year when Leif the Lucky, son of Erik the Red, first set foot on the country he called Vinland, which was probably Newfoundland, Canada.

Galleon

Fastest under sail
The swiftest sailing vessel is the *Yellow Pages Endeavour*, a trimaran with three short hulls and a sail that is 40 ft. (12 m)

high. In 1993 the vessel managed a speed of 46½ knots (86.2 km/h) at Sandy Point, Australia.

First submarine strike
The *Hunley*, a Confederate submarine, sunk a Union sloop in 1864, during the Civil War (1861–65). It rammed a torpedo attached to a harpoonlike bow into the enemy's wooden hull, released a 150-ft. (45-m) rope, withdrew, and then tightened the rope to activate the explosive. It was not until World War I (1914–18) that another submarine sank a ship in battle.

Water speed record
The hydroplane *Spirit of Australia* set the water speed record in 1978. The craft, driven by Ken Warby, reached a speed of 276 knots (511.1 km/h). However, Warby accelerated to about 300 knots (555 km/h) on another occasion the previous year, but officials were not present to witness the record.

Biggest warships
The world's largest warships are aircraft carriers owned by the U.S. Navy. They are seven *Nimitz Class* carriers, the biggest of which are 1,092 ft. (333 m) long. These vast floating runways can carry almost 100 aircraft.

Biggest submarines
The largest submarines ever built belonged to the Russian *Typhoon* class. *Typhoons* are 563 ft. (172 m) in length, are powered by twin nuclear reactors, and can travel at 25 knots (46 km/h) when submerged.

Biggest cargo ships
The *Jahre Viking* of Norway is the world's largest ship. The vessel is a supertanker and is 1,503 ft. (458 m) in length and 226 ft. (69 m) wide. It takes about five minutes to walk from the bow (front) of the ship to the stern (rear).

Container capacity
Big container ships can carry up to 2,700 separate containers. If you stacked them all one on top of the other, they would reach the height of Mount Everest.

Longest yachts
Abdul Aziz, the yacht of the Saudi Arabian royal family, is 482 ft. (147 m) long.

Rowing the Atlantic
In 1997, two New Zealanders, Phil Stubbs and Robert Hamill, rowed across the Atlantic Ocean in 41 days, beating the previous record by 32 days.

On the tracks

Largest steam engine
The biggest, heaviest, and most powerful steam engines in the world are the "Big Boys" (see page 81). The enormous engines weigh about 500 tons and were built to pull freight trains across Utah. The locomotives were 131¼ ft. (40 m) long, and the driving wheel was 5¾ ft. (1.8 m) in diameter. The firebox alone was large enough for a family dining room.

Fastest steam engine
The British Mallard (see page 81), with its sleek streamlined body, is the fastest-ever steam locomotive in the world. In 1938, it reached 126 mph (201 km/h) on a special journey along the main line between London and Edinburgh.

SD40-2

Largest diesel engine
The longest diesel engines run in the U.S. They work on the Union Pacific Railroad, are almost 100 ft. (30 m) long, and weigh 229 tons.

Largest freight train
Probably the longest-ever freight train was made up of 500 coal cars and ran on Ohio's Norfolk and Western Railroad in 1967. The train was pulled by six diesel locomotives and was 4 mi. (6.4 km) in length.

Longest rail tunnel
The world's longest rail tunnel connects the Japanese islands of Honshu and Hokkaido. The tunnel is 33 mi. (53 km) long, and most of it runs under water.

Largest rail station
New York's Grand Central Station is the world's largest. It has 44 platforms.

Widest track
Some of the world's widest trains run on track with a gauge (width) of 5½ ft. (1.676 m). This gauge is used in China, India, Pakistan, Spain, Portugal, and Argentina.

Fastest modern train
Of the world's various high-speed train services, the current record-holder is a French TGV (Train à Grande Vitesse). In 1990, the TGV (see page 86) reached 320 mph (515 km/h) near Vendôme. In normal service, however, TGVs run more slowly, with speeds averaging 132 mph (212 km/h) along much of the Paris-Lyon route.

In the air

Flexwing Microlight

First transatlantic solo flight
Charles Lindbergh, a pilot from Detroit, Michigan, made the first solo transatlantic flight in 1927. The journey took just 33 hours in Lindbergh's Ryan monoplane, The Spirit of St. Louis. The first nonstop transatlantic crossing (from Newfoundland to Ireland) had been achieved by British pilots John Alcock and Arthur Brown in 1919.

Fastest aircraft
The fastest aircraft of all was the Lockheed SR-71 of 1964. Its top speed was 2,193 mph (3,530 km/h) and it was said to be able to fly as high as 30,000 ft. (98,000 ft).

Fastest airliner
The BAC/Aérospatiale Concorde is the world's fastest airliner (see page 107). It reaches 1,450 mph (2,333 km/h)—2.2 times the speed of sound.

Biggest aircraft
The Airbus Super Transport A300-600 Beluga is the world's largest cargo-carrying aircraft. Its vast cargo compartment has a volume of 49,440 sq ft (1,400 sq m) and a length of 124 ft (37.7 m).

Biggest wingspan
The airplane with the longest wingspan was the Hughes H4 Hercules, a flying boat that was also nicknamed the "Spruce Goose." This massive aircraft, which was intended for the US government by American businessman Howard Hughes, had a wingspan of 320 ft (97.5 m). The plane, which cost $40 million to build, was only flown for a single test flight.

Largest airship
The biggest of the great airships was the German hydrogen-filled Hindenburg. Completed in March 1936, the Hindenburg took 10 days to travel around the world and made some 20 crossings of the Atlantic before it caught fire in May 1937, killing many of those on board.

Smallest airplane
The smallest working, human-piloted airplane was Bumble Bee Two. This tiny single-seater was just 9 ft. (2.7 m) long and had a wingspan of 5.5 ft. (1.7 m). The plane, built by Robert Tempe of Arizona, crashed in 1988.

Human-powered flight
In 1979, the first successful human-powered series, the Gossamer Albatross, flew across the English Channel. The flight finally fulfilled a dream of human-powered flight that had begun with the first experimental flying machines of the 19th century.

First strap-on personal helicopter
This could be the SoloTrek currently being developed with help from NASA (the American space agency). It straps on the back of the wearer to fly at speeds of 75 mph (120 km/h) over a range of 155 mi. (250 km).

In space

First living creature in space
The first live creature in space was not a person but a dog. The animal, named Laika, went into space in the Russian Sputnik 2 in 1957, shortly after the launch of Sputnik 1, the first artificial earth-orbiting satellite.

Shortest space flight
In May 1961, the American astronaut Alan Shepard made the briefest manned space flight on board Freedom 7. Shepard's spacecraft did not go into orbit, but flew in a huge curve, landing some 15 minutes after it took off. But it did leave the Earth's atmosphere and made Shepard the second man in space after Russia's Yuri Gagarin.

First space probe on another planet
The Russian probe Venera 7 was the first space probe to land on another planet. The craft landed on the planet Venus in 1970.

Fastest speed
The fastest-ever speed reached by a human being is 24,791 mph (39,897 km/h). It was achieved by the American astronauts of Apollo 10 when they returned to Earth in May 1969.

Longest continuous time in space
Russian Valeriy Poliyakov spent 437 days, 17 hours, 58 minutes, and 16 seconds from January 1994 to March 1995 on two Soyuz spacecrafts and the space station, Mir (see page 129).

Hubble Space Telescope

Glossary of Transportation Terms

Accelerator
A control, usually a pedal on a car, that allows you to increase or reduce the speed of the engine.

Aerodynamics
The study of the movement of objects through a gas; in road transportation, usually used to cut down friction and make vehicles more efficient.

Aft
Toward the rear of a vessel or aircraft.

Aileron
Flap on an airplane wing that the pilot can move to cause the aircraft to roll left or right and enter a turn.

Air brakes
Brakes that work using compressed air, used by trucks and trains.

Airbag
Safety device in a car, consisting of a bag that inflates with air to provide a cushion for the driver or passengers in a crash.

Air-cushion vehicle
A hovercraft that glides over land or water on a layer of compressed air.

Airship
Lighter-than-air aircraft with a gas-filled balloonlike envelope, an engine, and a steering mechanism.

Alcohol
Used in many rockets as a fuel; and, in Brazil, as an alternative fuel to gasoline to run cars.

Alloy
Substance made by mixing two or more metals to improve strength or hardness.

Amphibious
Capable of traveling both on land and in water.

Articulated
Containing a joint; an articulated semi has its front section joined to the rear by a flexible link that makes it easier to maneuver.

Axle
Rod passing through the center of a wheel, allowing the wheel to turn.

Barge
A flat-bottomed vessel, mainly for carrying freight, used mainly on rivers and canals; also a ceremonial boat.

Barque
Three- or four-masted ship with the mizzen- (rear) mast rigged with sails positioned fore-and-aft and the other masts square-rigged.

Barquentine
Three-masted ship with the main- and mizzen- (rear) masts fore-and-aft rigged, and the fore-mast square rigged.

BHP   *See* brake horsepower.

Biplane
Airplane with twin wings, one above the other.

Blimp
Small airship that does not have a rigid frame, often used for advertising.

Boat
Any small, water-going vessel, powered by oars, sails, or motor.

Boiler
Container in which water is boiled to produce steam in a steam engine.

Brake horsepower (BHP)
Unit of measurement of the effective power of an engine, measured by calculating the force applied to a brake by the engine drive shaft in a special testing machine (*see also* horsepower).

Bridge
Place on a ship from which the captain controls the vessel.

Broadside
All the guns of a ship that can be fired together in the same direction.

Buggy
Lightweight horsedrawn carriage; or small vehicle used for recreation.

Bulkhead
Dividing partition wall inside a ship or aircraft.

Bullet train
Very fast bullet-nosed train as used on the Japanese *Shinkansen* network.

Cab
Part of a truck or train engine that accommodates the driver or engineer.

Caravel
Light sailing ship used between the 14th and 17th centuries.

Carbon fiber
Very strong, lightweight material used in making many items related to transportation, from turbine blades to high-performance boats.

Cargo
Goods carried by a truck, cargo ship, or freight train.

Carrack
Large trading ship used between the 14th and 16th centuries.

Catamaran
Ship or boat with twin hulls.

Chassis
Supporting frame and wheels of a motor vehicle or carriage.

Clipper
Tall-masted cargo-carrying sailing ship of the 19th century, capable of very fast sea journeys.

Cockpit
Part of an aircraft, spacecraft, racing car, and powerboat where the captain, pilot, or driver sits.

Cog
North European cargo ship of the Middle Ages with a single mast and square sail.

Commuter train
Train used by people traveling to work, usually from the outskirts to the center of a large city.

Composites
Plastics, such as carbon fiber, which are used in vehicle construction. Alloys, which are also used, are metals.

Conning tower
Upward-pointing structure on a submarine used for navigation and as the entrance to the vessel.

Container
A standard-sized steel box used on many ships, trucks, and trains for carrying cargo.

Convertible
Car with a roof, often made of fabric, that can be folded back or taken off.

Corsair
Pirate, especially one from North Africa; or the vessel sailed by such a person.

Coupé
Two-door car with a roof that has a marked downward slope toward the back.

Cowcatcher
Structure on the front of a locomotive designed to sweep obstructions off the track.

Craft
General term for any ship or boat, or any air or space vehicle.

Crew
Group of people who work on board a ship or aircraft, under the command of the captain.

Cylinder
Tube-shaped part of an engine, in which a piston moves up and down.

Deck
One of the horizontal floors of a ship or aircraft.

Derailleur
Gearing system used on bicycles, in which the chain can be shifted from one drive cog to another.

Diesel engine
Type of internal combustion engine in which the fuel ignites because it is injected directly into the cylinder when the air has been compressed to high pressure.

Dirigible
Craft, usually an airship, that can be steered, rather than just drifting like a free balloon.

Drag
The force that tends to slow down any vehicle traveling through air or water.

Engine
Mechanical device that powers a ship, car, train, or other vehicle.

Exhaust
Waste gases produced by an engine. Also, the part of the engine through which the waste emissions pass.

Ferry
Vessel that carries passengers (and often vehicles) back and forth across a stretch of water.

Fiberglass
Lightweight material made by molding a mat or cloth of thin glass fibers in a plastic matrix. Used in some car bodies and the hulls of some boats; also called glass-fiber or GRP (glass-reinforced plastic).

Fore
Toward the front of a vessel or aircraft.

Four-stroke cycle
Most gasoline and diesel engines operate on this cycle of strokes (the up and down movements) of the pistons.

Four-wheel drive (4WD)
Type of motor vehicle in which the power of the engine is transferred to all four wheels (rather than the standard two), to provide good traction on difficult ground.

Freight
Cargo or goods. A freighter is a cargo vessel.

Friction
Resistance felt when one surface rubs against another.

Galleon
Large sailing ship with high fore and after castles, used in the 15th and 16th centuries.

Gallon
Nonmetric measurement of capacity equivalent to approximately 3.75 liters.

Gauge
Measurement of the distance between a pair of train wheels or rails. This varies around the world: the standard gauge in North America, most of Western Europe, and China is 56½ in. (143.5 cm).

Gears
System of cogs that transmits the motion of the engine to the wheels of a motor vehicle and which can change the speed and torque available.

Glider
Aircraft designed in a similar way to an airplane, but without an engine. Very efficient aerodynamic design allows it to stay airborne using natural upcurrents.

Hatchback
Car with a sloping rear door that opens upward.

Haul
To pull, to transport, or (of a ship) to change direction.

Helium
A very light, chemically inert gas often used in airships.

Horsepower (HP)
Measurement of power, roughly equivalent to the strength of one horse.

Hovercraft
Vessel supported by a cushion of air, capable of traveling over land and sea.

HPV (Human Powered Vehicle)
Any human-powered transportation including bicycle-style vehicles.

Hull
Body of a ship.

Hydrofoil
Vessel with winglike structures under the hull called foils that develop lift and raise the hull out of the water as it travels.

Hydrogen
A very light, highly flammable gas that was once used in balloons and airships.

Jet engine
Engine that uses the momentum of a jet of hot exhaust gas to propel an airplane or other vehicle.

139

Juggernaut
A term (of Hindu origin) sometimes used to describe a very large truck.

Jumbo jet
Large, wide-bodied airliner.

Jump jet
Fighter airplane that can take off and land vertically.

Keel
Main structural part of a ship that stretches along the whole of the bottom of the vessel; it may also protrude down into the water to help make the vessel more stable.

Kilowatt
Unit of power now replacing horsepower in automotive engineering.

Knot
Measurement of speed equivalent to 1 nautical mile per hour (1.853184 km/h).

Lift
Force needed to raise an aircraft into the air.

Liner
Large vessel that carries passengers.

Liter
Standard metric measurement of capacity.

Locomotive
The engine unit of a railroad train.

Mach
A measurement of an aircraft's speed compared to the speed of sound. Mach 1 means the plane is traveling at the speed of sound; Mach 2 means twice the speed of sound. At sea level the speed of sound is 758 mph (1,220 km/h), but it is slower the higher you go.

Machine gun
Automatic gun that can fire many bullets at high speed, attached to tanks, fighter aircraft, bombers, and other military vehicles. Also carried by infantry.

Magnet
Piece of iron that attracts other metals containing iron.

Maneuver
Intricate movement of vehicle that requires skill to achieve.

Marshaling yard
Area containing many linked railroad tracks, where rail cars are sorted and joined together to form trains.

Mass production
Method of making objects in large numbers using standard, repetitive processes, as with the modern automobile.

Mast
Vertical structure or pole that carries a ship's sails, or other equipment in powered vessels.

Merchant ship
Vessel designed to carry goods, particularly from one country to another.

Metro
Underground railroad system serving a town or city. Called subway in the U.S.

Microlight
Very small, lightweight airplane.

Module
Single part that can be interchanged with other parts of the same size.

Monorail
Railroad that travels on a single rail.

Nozzle
Outlet tube or spout; pipe through which fuel enters a cylinder in an internal combustion engine. Also exit zone of jet or rocket engine.

Nuclear power
Power generated as a result of a nuclear reaction. The heat of the nuclear reaction is used to create steam and drive a turbine.

Orbit
Circular path around a planet or moon followed by a spacecraft or satellite, or by one astronomical body around another.

Outrigger
Stabilizing framework or structure sticking out from one side of a boat; or, a boat with such a structure to increase stability.

Oxidizer
Chemical supplied to a rocket engine that helps the fuel to burn.

Paddle
Short oar, normally used in a canoe.

Pantograph
Metal framework fitted on top of an electric locomotive or tram, to pick up current from overhead wires.

Piston
Cylindrical component that moves up and down inside the cylinder of an engine.

Pneumatic tire
Vehicle tire filled with compressed air.

Probe
Vehicle used for space exploration; particularly an unmanned vehicle sent to one of the planets or to travel outside the solar system.

Propeller
Device made up of a shaft and several specially shaped blades, used to drive a ship or airplane; also called a screw.

Prototype
The first finished example of a vehicle, built as a one-off, before regular production begins and from which later examples can be copied.

Pullman
Railroad car with comfortable accommodations for both sitting and for sleeping.

Rack and pinion
Steering mechanism used in many cars, in which a toothed wheel (the pinion) engages with a toothed bar (the rack).

Radar
System that uses reflected radio waves to detect invisible objects, such as aircraft in the sky or ships at sea; it is also used by pilots and sailors to work out their own position. The word radar comes from the phrase "Radio Detection And Ranging."

Reconnaissance
A first survey of an area to learn its features; air forces or navies may use specialized reconnaissance aircraft or ships to check for enemy positions.

Rickshaw
Small carriage with two wheels, pulled by a person or by someone riding a bicycle.

Rig
The arrangement of sails on a boat or ship.

Rigging
The ropes that hold up a ship's masts and control its sails.

Rolling stock
Railroad vehicles—including locomotives, cars, and freight wagons.

Rotor
Arrangement of spinning blades on a helicopter.

Rudder
Movable flap for steering a boat or aircraft.

Rush hour
Time when most people are traveling to and from work, school, and so on.

Saloon
Cabin on a boat where people relax and eat their meals.

Satellite
Object that orbits a planet.

Schooner
Two-masted ship, with sails rigged fore-and-aft.

Ship
Any large seagoing vessel.

Shunting
Moving railroad rolling stock from one line to another.

Skidoo
Vehicle used in snow, with caterpillar tracks at the rear and steerable skis at the front.

Sled
Vehicle with sliding runners, usually used to travel across snow, also called a sleigh.

Smokestack
Chimney of a steam locomotive.

Solar power
Energy generated using the rays of the sun.

Stacking
System whereby air traffic control keeps planes waiting to land, circling above at fixed heights.

Station wagon
Car with a rear door opening onto an area behind the seats designed to carry luggage or other goods.

Stratosphere
Part of the atmosphere, beginning from 5–10 m. (8–16 km) above the Earth's surface.

Streamlined
Designed with a sleek, aerodynamic body, so that drag is kept low.

Submersible
Small submarine used for exploration and other nonmilitary work.

Supersonic
Faster than the speed of sound.

Suspension
System of springs and other devices that support a vehicle's body on its axles and is designed to cushion those traveling inside from bumps on the ground.

Tail
Flat part of an aircraft's tail, designed to make the craft more stable in flight.

Tanker
Vessel or vehicle in which most of the body is made up of large tanks for carrying liquids in bulk.

Tender
Rear part of a steam locomotive, carrying supplies of coal and water.

Thermals
Currents of warm air on which gliders soar.

Thrust
Pushing force produced by a jet engine or rocket that moves the craft forward.

Tiller
Lever used to control a boat's rudder.

Tolls
Barriers with booths collecting payments to use a stretch of road, canal, or bridge.

Ton
Measurement of weight equaling 2,000 lb (907 kg).

Torpedo
Self-propelled underwater weapon that explodes when it hits the target.

Tram
Passenger-carrying vehicle that runs along rails on a road.

Transmission
System (consisting of gearbox and clutch) that transfers power from a motor vehicle's engine to its wheels.

Trolley
Device, fitted to a trolleybus, that picks up electric power from overhead wires.

Tug
Ship that tows other vessels.

Turbine
Motor which uses a bladed wheel that is turned by the force of water, steam, or burning gas.

Turbo (turbocharger)
Type of turbine fitted to a vehicle engine; it supplies air under pressure to the engine's cylinders for better performance.

Turbofan
Jet engine that uses a large fan to increase the thrust at lower speeds suited to civil aircraft.

Turbojet
Gas turbine engine that propels an aircraft by its high-speed exhaust. A turboprop powers a propeller.

Vessel
Any ship, boat, or water-borne transportation.

Wagon
Railroad truck for carrying freight; or, a four-wheeled horse-drawn vehicle, especially for carrying goods.

Wind tunnel
Device for producing a steady stream of air, used for testing the aerodynamics of cars, aircraft, and other vehicles.

Wingspan
Tip-to-tip length of an aircraft's wings.

Index

Acknowledgments

Kinsey & Harrison would like to thank:
John W. Walker, Director at TAL Management Ltd., Hampshire, England (for Cable & Wireless Adventurer); Tim Cley at Reynard Motorsports Ltd, Oxon (for Indy cars); Bart Garbrecht, President at CEO P.R.O.P Tour, Inc., Lake Hamilton, Florida, USA (for F1 powerboats); Cameron Kellegher at HSBC and Jaguar Racing (for F1 cars); Ford/Pivco Industries AS (for Th!nk car); Pegasus Aviation; Jason Lewis at www.goals.com; Robert Dane and Mark Gold at www.solarsailor.com.

Artwork credits
t = top; b = bottom; l = left; r = right; c = center

Tony Bryan: 32–33; 36–37; 104–5; 106–7; 108–9; 112–13. Peter Bull: 16–17; 46–47; 48–49; 50–51; 52–53; 54–55; 58–59; 60–61; 64–65; 66–67; 68–69; 70–71; 72b; 76–77; 86–87; 100–101; 102–103; 111tl; 116b; 130c. Mark Franklin: 10–11; 14–15; 18–19; 20–21; 22–23; 24–25; 26–27; 30–31; 34–35; 38–39; 42–43; 126–27. John Lawson: 28–29; 62–63. Simon Roulstone: 12–13; 40–41; 78–79; 80–81; 82–83; 84–85; 88–89; 90–91; 92–93; 94–95; 114–15; 120–21; 122–23; 124–25; 128–29. Peter Sarson: 130tr.

Photographic Credits
t = top; b = bottom; l = left; r = right; c = center

6/7 Robert Harding Picture Library/Ian Griffiths; 28 AllSport/Mark Thompson; 8l Corbis/Hulton Deutsch Collection, 8/9t Science & Society Picture Library/Science Museum, 8/9b Science & Society Picture Library/Science Museum, 9t,c Bryan & Cherry Alexander, 9b Dyson Industries Ltd; 44/45 The Stock Market; 63 Ajax Silver Image Picture Library; 72l Popperfoto, 72r Corbis/Bettmann, 73t Kos Picture Source, 73c Seaco Picture Library, 73b Kos Picture Source; 74/75 The Stock Market; 86 Milepost 921/2; 96l Corbis/Nik Wheeler, 96r Ford/Pirco Industries AS, 96/97t Solar Sailor/Cannings Australia, 96/97b Popperfoto/Mark Baker, 97 Corbis/Michael S. Yamashita; 98/99 Robert Harding Picture Library; 100 NASA; 102 Corbis/Bettmann; 116 gettyone Stone; 117tl Milepost 921/2/Colin Garratt, 117tr Corbis/Roger Wood 117bl Corbis/Gunter Marx, 117br Corbis/Neil Beer; 118/119, 126 NASA; 130 Popperfoto/NASA, 130/131 Royal Geographical Society, 131t NASA, 131b Novosti (London).

Every effort has been made to trace the copyright holders. Marshall Editions apologizes for any unintentional omissions and would be pleased, in such cases, to add an acknowledgement in future editions.